A KIDS' GUIDE TO THE
AMERICAN REVOLUTION

KATHLEEN KRULL
★ ILLUSTRATED BY ANNA DIVITO ★

HARPER
An Imprint of HarperCollinsPublishers

Library of Congress Control Number: 2017951333

ISBN 978-0-06-238110-1 (trade bdg.) — ISBN 978-0-06-238109-5 (pbk.)

Typography by Chelsea C. Donaldson

19 20 21 22 CG/LSCH 10 9 8 7 6 5 4 3

❖

First Edition

To patriotic revolutionaries Dr. Jacqui Ignatova
and Dr. Anatoli Ignatov

—K. K.

For Claire Oyster

—A. D.

CONTENTS

INTRODUCTION

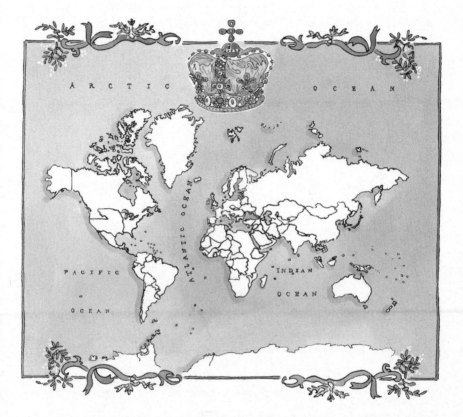

The Birth of a New Nation

Oceans of words have been devoted to the American Revolution. It's a gigantic, complex topic—how do we boil it all down?

First off, our War for Independence was basically a blowup between a parent figure and unruly children. Thirteen colonies, so new they didn't quite know what they were doing, blew up against a mighty kingdom, resenting its reign.

The colonists were unhappy with the king's treatment of them
and eventually had to rebel.

Okay, it was a lot more complicated than a blowup. Considerably more deadly, messy, scary, and supenseful. This was a blowup that exploded on the world stage, affecting all of history afterward.

The war itself was not a straightforward thing. It

wasn't that one day—*bam*—war was declared. Leading up to it was a long, incredibly annoying series of insults and injuries between the two parties, mostly against the colonies. It lacked a clear-cut beginning or even an end—and the Declaration of Independence, one of its most electric moments, was sort of in the middle.

★ ★ ★ ★ ★ ★ ★ ★ ★ ★ ★ ★ ★ ★ ★ ★ ★ ★ ★ ★

WISE WORDS

"The Revolution was in the minds and hearts of the people. . . . Thirteen clocks were made to strike together—a perfection of mechanism, which no artist had ever before effected."

—John Adams, 1818

★ ★ ★ ★ ★ ★ ★ ★ ★ ★ ★ ★ ★ ★ ★ ★ ★ ★ ★ ★

The Revolutionary War was the opposite of a fair fight. It was very David against Goliath, an underdog versus a superpower. On one side was the kingdom of Great Britain. It combined two very old, very well-established countries—England (founded in 1066) and Scotland (founded in 843). Once they joined together in 1707, they plotted world domination, intent on growing into the mighty British Empire.

Great Britain had the most sophisticated and well-supplied army and navy in the world. They had been exploring and colonizing up a storm—areas around the Caribbean, parts of Canada, and parts of Africa. As of 1775, Britain ruled over some eight million subjects. The British began to brag that the Empire owned so much of the earth that "the sun never set" on its people.

The American colonies were a moneymaker for the Empire, planned as its cornerstone—a crown jewel, in fact, with their wildly abundant natural resources and theoretically grateful colonists.

All the Sources of Money

To the British, the colonies were the entry point to some 950 million acres in what would later become the lower 48 states. An entry, in fact, into a seemingly unlimited source of money. This was clean, unpolluted land with unparalleled resources—forests dense with valuable timber, rivers with glittery fish all but jumping ashore, wild animals to be hunted for their precious furs, mines producing coal and iron. In a generally mild climate, the fertile land was perfect for farming crops and raising livestock. Early industries benefiting Britain included whaling, shipbuilding, and production of alcohol. On top of all that, America would supply an ever-expanding market for its own goods. The trading possibilities were endless.

Meanwhile, on the other side of the war—and the Atlantic Ocean—were the brand-new colonies. They had begun forming only as of 1607, and by the time of the Revolutionary War had about 2.5 million people, of which half a million were slaves. They were far from united, with no one official government. They had no navy. For an army, there were only ill-trained volunteers in various colonies' militias.

This blowup could have gone so, so bad.

AN INSULT FROM SOMEONE IN ENGLAND WHO ACTUALLY LIKED AMERICA

"In all laws relating to trade and navigation especially, this is the mother country, [Americans] are the children; they must obey, and we prescribe."

—Lord William Pitt, 1770

The Revolution is a mountainous, multifaceted topic that scholars can spend years exploring. This book doesn't cover every battle—or it would be too heavy to lift—but it attempts to tell you what you need to know to understand the Revolution's meaning, its place in history, and the birth of our country.

DOING THE MATH

Benjamin Franklin, one of the most brilliant minds in the colonies, looked at how fast the American population was growing and did some calculations. He figured out that the population was doubling every 20 years, even without new immigrants. So it would overtake Great Britain's in a hundred years. (He was correct, as usual.) Technically, the colonies could have overthrown their governing country one day through sheer manpower. But until then—what?

The war gave us heroes, our first president, and much, much more.

Most momentously, it bequeathed to us the Declaration of Independence, one of the most remarkable documents in history. It spelled out the reasons *why* the colonists had to rebel against the mother country and begin to govern themselves. It's not exaggerating things to say that the Declaration launched America. It gave us our whole idea of what we were to be—something the world hadn't yet seen.

★ ★ ★ ★ ★ ★ ★ ★ ★ ★ ★ ★ ★ ★ ★

WISE WORDS

"Our nation was born right here in Philadelphia. Our Declaration of Independence and Constitution were signed just a few blocks away. And ever since—even through dark and difficult chapters of our history—the idea of America has shone through. At our best, we are, as Robert Kennedy said, 'a great country, an unselfish country, and a compassionate country.'"

—Secretary of State Hillary Clinton, 2016 speech

★ ★ ★ ★ ★ ★ ★ ★ ★ ★ ★ ★ ★ ★ ★

You will find out that the Revolutionary War changed—in a word—everything. But to start at the beginning with one nearly insurmountable problem: How were thirteen very different colonies going to unite into one country?

CHAPTER 1

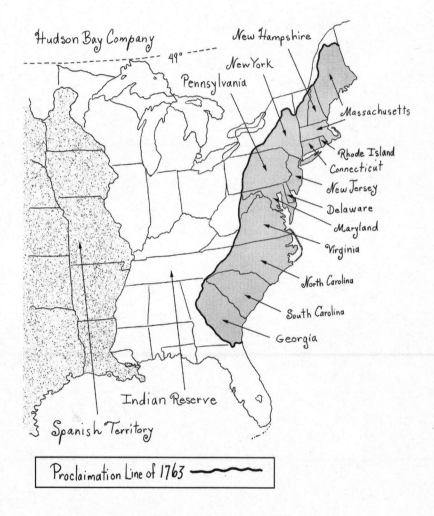

Hudson Bay Company

49°

New Hampshire

New York

Pennsylvania

Massachusetts

Rhode Island

Connecticut

New Jersey

Delaware

Maryland

Virginia

North Carolina

South Carolina

Georgia

Indian Reserve

Spanish Territory

Proclaimation Line of 1763

The Notorious Thirteen Colonies

A colony is not a country. It's a parcel of land governed by some other country. The relationship between a colony and its ruler is by its very nature unequal, unfair—a child versus a parent.

During the European colonial period, which lasted centuries, the major countries of Europe—notably Spain, France, and Great Britain—got busy colonizing. They established colonies in Asia and Africa, and—once it was "discovered" in 1492—the New World of the Americas.

New settlers had to find ways to work with the Indians
when they came to the colonies.

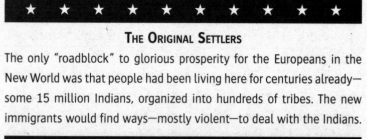

THE ORIGINAL SETTLERS

The only "roadblock" to glorious prosperity for the Europeans in the New World was that people had been living here for centuries already—some 15 million Indians, organized into hundreds of tribes. The new immigrants would find ways—mostly violent—to deal with the Indians.

What would become the country of America was just ripe for European colonization. Spain and France and other countries put up their flags here, and the British began streaming in as of 1607, all the immigrants risking their lives in search of religious freedom and a better life.

By 1732, there were thirteen colonies governed by Great Britain. All were quite different, and it was each colony for itself—there were no common bonds.

Here are the thirteen American colonies in order of their establishment:

Virginia: Settlers arrived in Jamestown in 1607, establishing the first British colony in the New World. It became the richest and the one with the most people, and it was the first colony to elect representatives to its governing body, the House of Burgesses. Virginia was dependent on slave labor and on a single crop—tobacco—which made some planters very wealthy, able to live like the British aristocrats they'd left back home. White settlers were outnumbered by their slaves, and the majority of them were members of the Church of England, the national church of the mother country.

Massachusetts: Puritans escaping persecution founded this colony in 1630. They believed that the Church of England needed to be "purified" of its Roman Catholic influences. It became the most rebellious colony of all, home to an organization called the Sons of Liberty, and its capital, Boston, was known as the Cradle of Liberty.

New Hampshire: One colony not founded by religious dissenters (though it had a significant Scotch-Irish population who were Presbyterian) was New Hampshire. People were drawn here in response to advertisements of its abundant fishing, farmland, and forests. An assertively independent place, New Hampshire was the first colony to establish a government independent of Britain. Later it chose its bold motto, "Live Free or Die," after a statement made by its best-known soldier of the war—"Live free or die: Death is not the worst of evils."

Maryland: Originally a refuge for Catholics, who were unpopular—hated, actually—in England, Maryland became an early headquarters for religious tolerance and diversity, and is considered America's birthplace for religious freedom.

Connecticut: This colony was founded to escape *Puritan* intolerance, with people moving here for religious freedom and for the fertile land. It had the first written state constitution allowing the people to govern themselves, and later contributed many soldiers and supplies to the American side of the war.

Rhode Island: The smallest colony, also founded to escape Puritan intolerance, welcomed people of any religion, including the local Indian religions and people with no religion at all. With its tradition of independent thinking, this was the first colony to renounce its loyalty to Britain, in response to taxes being imposed on sugar, the main ingredient for its rum trade.

Delaware: First settled by the Dutch, with strong ties to Britain, Delaware was dependent on its tobacco crop and the labor of slaves and indentured servants.

North Carolina: A place of religious tolerance, North Carolina was a tobacco-growing colony with slaves and even more indentured servants—these were people so desperate to escape their harsh lives in the Old World that they signed contracts promising to work for four to ten years in order to pay for their passage to the colonies.

South Carolina: Also a place of religious tolerance, South Carolina became a colony where the majority of the population was slaves, brought in from the West Coast of Africa to grow rice and precious indigo (the source of blue dye), enriching British planters. Charleston was the leading port and center of trade in the South.

New York: This was established by Dutch, German, Scottish, and English settlers—many with strong ties to Britain. The dominant religion of New York City was still the Church of England, but the city was evolving into a cosmopolitan hub attracting people of different religions and nationalities. Strong opposition to British rule was growing. One-third of the battles in the war were fought here.

New Jersey: With a rapidly growing population attracted by fertile lands and religious tolerance, New Jersey was known as the Crossroads of the Revolution because so many battles took place there, like the Battle of Trenton and the Battle of Princeton.

Pennsylvania: This colony was home to the largest

city and the capital at the time, Philadelphia. The city was Quaker-dominated but sophisticated, full of people of all religions and speaking many languages. It was the most influential of all the colonies and the strongest voice at first for reconciling with Britain—the population included many still loyal to the king and many who just wanted to stay out of the conflict.

Georgia: Named for King George's father, with a governor appointed by the king, Georgia was originally planned as a safe place to relocate British people who were in debt. In Britain, those who couldn't pay their bills were thrown into dungeon-like debtors prisons until they could come up with the money—a nearly impossible feat while imprisoned. After its establishment in 1732, Georgia soon began attracting a wide mix of people, but it was plagued by attacks from pirates and by Spain. The people there were poorer than those in other colonies and had smaller farms.

★ ★ ★ ★ ★ ★ ★ ★ ★ ★

A LESSER-KNOWN USE OF THE THIRTEEN COLONIES

Among many of its benefits, the colonies were a place for Great Britain to unload its "undesirables." By this time, it was shipping 1,000 convicts a year to our shores. Many were guilty only of being in debt. Great Britain was also happy to get rid of religious dissidents who opposed the Church of England, its official religion, with their strange ideas. All in all, the British had reasons to look down on the unruly hordes who left its shores—and look down they did—but that didn't stop the steady river of immigrants in search of a better life from coming to the colonies either.

★ ★ ★ ★ ★ ★ ★ ★ ★ ★

Not Much in Common

Colonists didn't necessarily know people from other colonies. With no good roads, travel was a serious challenge. Often colonists didn't even particularly like people from the other colonies. They were suspicious of one another's different religions, accents, attitudes toward slavery, customs, foods, and even smells.

Each colony took care of itself, with its own laws and governing body. Deciding things locally, through town meetings, seemed best.

And things were mostly working out very well indeed. In this new lush land—once they took it from the Indians already living there—white colonists were thriving. Businesses flourished—fur-trading, printing, shipbuilding, fishing, and skilled crafts-men making all kinds of household objects. Farms produced like mad—fruits, vegetables, tobacco, rice. Many people were making money, achieving a higher standard of living than they ever could have reached in Great Britain or Europe. Everyone worked hard, even children, who were less protected and had more responsibilities in the colonies than they'd had in the Old World.

As a bonus, colonists didn't have to pay money directly to the British government as a tax.

Taxes

Taxes are money that you've earned going to the government to pay for the services it provides its citizens. No one exists who actually *likes* being taxed, but many early Americans came from places where taxes made rulers rich and kept poor people poor. The colonists had come to America to get away from such corrupt systems.

Colonists of many trades were thriving in the New World.

Actually, up until 1763 Britain had neglected the colonies, and colonists liked it that way. They weren't used to being told what to do. So when the "mother country" started bossing them around, there were many fiery debates, and ultimately more and more colonists decided they had to resist the new rules. The people wanted to govern themselves—a shocking proposition at the time.

The American Revolution, also known as the War for Independence, was going to pit a bunch of underdressed and underfed farmers against well-fed, armed-to-the-teeth professional soldiers.

At no time did the colonists know for sure what the outcome of the war would be. At so many points along the way, they could have lost the war and lost *everything*. And the consequences of losing were dire. The punishment for treason—the overthrow of the British government—was death, sometimes in very bloody ways. The suspense of this war would have been enough to crush weaker people.

But the colonists were different from those who had stayed behind. Dreaming delicious dreams of prosperity and freedom, they had braved a dangerous voyage— at least a month if all went well—as they sailed out of the Old World. It was not a journey for wimps—three thousand miles across the sea and into the frightening unknown territory of the New World.

So the colonists were already survivors. And they were younger and scrappier—the median age of the colonists was sixteen.

Yet it was going to take all their strength to endure that terrible suspense over the outcome of the war, which was going to last seven very long and painful years.

CHAPTER 2

King Louis XV

King George III

Inching Toward Revolution

The Revolutionary War didn't explode overnight. It was years in the making. In fact, it all began with *another* war. This was the French and Indian War, which started in 1754.

Despite its name, this was actually a war between Great Britain and France. Each wanted control over the continent of North America. The Indians, the original owners of the land, were aiding the vastly outnumbered French. Britain was aiding the colonists.

This war finally ended in 1763 with the British driving the French out, changing the continent forever. There were no more French colonies here after that, and Britain began tightening its rein on its own thirteen colonies.

INDIANS DURING THE REVOLUTIONARY WAR

Those who aren't Indian tend to lump Indians together, thinking they're all alike. But this is not the case. The Nations, or tribes, are all quite different. In this era they had different languages (dozens of them), spiritual beliefs, traditions, friends and enemies, attitudes toward women, attitudes toward colonists and the war.

Warring tribes could unite, if it served their purposes for trading or defense. The Iroquois Confederacy, for example, brought together six very different Nations—Mohawk, Oneida, Cayuga, Seneca, Onondaga, and Tuscarora. It flourished by uniting thousands of villages and taking care of the land together. Corn, the staple crop, was stored and distributed in an equal fashion by each clan's mothers, the oldest women in every family. In war, the Confederacy was much more effective than each tribe acting alone. But during the Revolutionary War, they chose different sides, eventually breaking up their alliance.

With the British flag now flying over so much of North America, most colonists seemed delighted, proud of the British victory and their own identity as "free Britons."

The rapidly growing American population now outnumbered Indians by twenty to one, making colonists ever bolder about taking over more land. White colonists looked forward to a time of uninterrupted peace with Europeans, expansion, and even more prosperity.

Americans appreciated Britain's support during the French and Indian War, but now felt like they could protect themselves. After all, they'd been the ones to take the land, clear the forest, erect the cities, build the homes, and raise huge families.

For protection, they could go back to relying on themselves, with each colony having its own part-time militia. This was a group of male civilians of all ages trained in using weapons. The youngest and strongest in the militias were chosen as minutemen—able to be ready to fight in sixty seconds. But technically the militias were more like police, keeping order, than an actual fighting army.

Colonial militias were made up of male citizens of all ages.

At this point, the colonists were like a sleeping giant about to be awakened into action by someone poking them. King George III, ruler of Great Britain, made the mistake of doing so.

King George Issues an Annoying Proclamation

It turned out Britain didn't see things the same way the colonists did. For one thing, they thought our makeshift militias were a joke compared to their extraordinarily well-trained troops. A British general reported back to London that our soldiers were "the dirtiest, most contemptible, cowardly dogs that you can conceive."

But there was more. The first hint of the clash to come was that October, with the Proclamation of 1763. In it, King George banned colonists from settling beyond the Appalachian Mountains (the barrier dividing the East Coast colonies from what would become the Midwest) or moving westward onto Indian lands. He even decreed that those who had already moved west had to move back east. Colonists were supposed to stick to exploring to the north—Nova Scotia—and south—Florida.

Why? The king wanted to restrict our borders so it would be easier to maintain political control over the colonies. He also wanted to put limits on westward settlement in order to avoid border conflicts with Indians, which were costly to him.

King George had never bothered to visit America and in fact had never left southern England. But that didn't stop him from meddling.

He shouldn't have been surprised at the rage that followed his Proclamation. Colonists were appalled that the new British policy seemed to side with the Indians and not with them. How dare King George interfere in the settlement of their new land from three thousand miles away?

KING GEORGE III—EVIL, INSANE, INCOMPETENT, OR WHAT?

King George had a strong sense of duty, and this
seemed to make him a tyrant.

Technically, the king probably wasn't evil. When the war began he was 37. He loved music and played violin and piano—a highlight of his life was seeing a young Mozart play the organ. A book lover, he had one of the best libraries in the world. He liked to putter around on his farms in old clothes. He was devoted to his wife and their 15 children.

He wasn't actually incompetent but perhaps a little insecure. His strongest trait was his sense of duty, and this seemed to make him a tyrant, or at least blind to the idea of compromise. Americans simply had to be made to obey. He was a king, after all, ruling by divine right. He spent hours every day in prayer.

It wasn't until his final years that he was called "Mad King

George"—a nickname some today have assumed applied to him during the war as well. But the rumors about him being mad or insane actually started years later, after the Revolution.

The king didn't send in enough troops to really enforce the Proclamation. But it still angered white American settlers, and they basically ignored it. They viewed Indians as obstacles in the way of their dreams of land ownership and wealth, and they resented what King George was trying to do.

Money Matters

The next move from King George III had to do with money. Thanks to the cost of raising, supplying, and funding an army on foreign soil, Britain had incurred the largest debt it had ever had—billions of dollars in today's money—all for the purpose of protecting the colonies during the French and Indian War that had just ended in 1763. It needed to raise money pronto, and it expected the colonists to shoulder some of the burden.

THE KING'S ADVISERS

King George did have help. He relied on Parliament, the branch of the British government that made laws and appointed advisers and military officers to help rule the kingdom. Parliament was dominated by members of the wealthy nobility, pompously arguing with one another at Westminster Palace in London. It had no members from the colonies—no Americans allowed.

The king's chief adviser, the head of the government, Lord Frederick North, was the prime minister during most of the war. Another lord described him as a "great, heavy, booby looking fellow." Lord North had a particularly belligerent stance toward the colonies, saying things like "America must fear you before she can love you."

The king took a moderate tone at first, assuming the colonists would see "that to be a subject of Great Britain, with all its consequences, is to be the freest member of any civil society in the known world."

But the colonists didn't see that at all. The "consequences," or benefits, were starting to be outweighed by the irritations.

Britain had nurtured and invested in the colonies and didn't want to take a chance that rebellion might be brewing.

No one on this side of the Atlantic had actually mentioned independence, but King George didn't want to take a chance that a rebellion might be brewing—after all Britain had done to nurture and invest in the colonies. In Parliament meetings, the colonists were insulted as "children planted by our Care, nourished up by our Indulgence ... protected by our Arms." The British didn't try to hide how much they looked down on Americans.

So in March of 1765 Parliament passed the Stamp Act.

Colonists Find a Point of Agreement

Without further ado, every paper item that was sold in the colonies had to have an official stamp, paid for with a tax.

That meant anything made of paper—books; invitations; diplomas; court documents, so legal business came to a standstill; and marriage certificates, so some put off their weddings. Newspapers, used to buying paper from Britain, had to scramble for other sources of paper in order to avoid the tax. Even playing cards. With only two paper mills in the colonies, paper went into short supply.

How Much Were the Stamps?

The tax imposed one shilling (about $5.87 in today's currency) per page and two shillings per advertisement, so a newspaper of 35 pages with ads would have the equivalent of some $300 tacked on to the price. A diploma or certificate printed on parchment would have an extra two pounds added—about $235. A deck of cards would cost an additional $6.00, while a calendar was a bargain at about $2.00.

The tax affected almost everyone. It was the first major tax imposed on the colonies, the first on items made in America, and it was incredibly unpopular.

Sending money right to the British government? No way. Outrage at the Stamp Act turned out to be the first thing that many people in the various colonies agreed on.

Lack of taxes was actually one reason why people had been prospering. Taxes in the colonies were few and far between. Some colonies charged a tax on land or property, as a source of revenue for the local government for roads, churches, and schools. But there was no tax on income.

Colonists considered it a basic right to make as much money as possible without giving any to a government. Bartering was popular, paying with crops or animal skins, with no money changing hands. They even tried to evade indirect taxes, such as the customs duty due on items imported from other countries. They thought nothing of avoiding customs by resorting to illegal smuggling, and the British hadn't been doing much to stop it.

People like wealthy Virginian plantation-owner George Washington were solidly pro-British until the Stamp Act came along. "They have no right to put their hands in my pockets," he fumed.

Others, like prominent scientist and statesman Benjamin Franklin, were also more or less pro-British until that point. Franklin opposed the Stamp Act, and while living in England, spoke out against it. He was powerless to prevent its passage and in fact recommended a friend to the job of distributing the stamps.

To people in his hometown of Philadelphia, his failure and job recommendation hinted that he was *pro* Stamp Act. A mob fell upon his fine house in Philly and threatened to destroy it; his wife, Deborah, had to defend it with guns. Franklin set to work arguing with Parliament into repealing, or taking back, the Stamp Act.

BENJAMIN FRANKLIN

Ben Franklin was a true American success story. After a tough childhood, he became such a profitable printer that he could retire at 42 and devote himself to his real love, science. Franklin danced through his long life as a statesman, author, publisher, scientist, inventor, and diplomat.

Internationally renowned as the first American scientist for his experiments with electricity, he was drafted to go to England as a sort of ambassador for the colonies. Starting in 1757, he spent a total of 15 years there, keeping up his scientific work and representing the colonies as best as he could. He tried to make sure Britain treated the colonists fairly—and at that he failed. He lacked any strong allies in Parliament. Also, at first he was too conciliatory, a little too agreeable, until the Stamp Act roused his ire.

Benjamin Franklin was well-known around the world for his experiments with electricity.

Under the Stamp Act, life in the colonies got more vexing. What other things were the British going to start taxing? Where would this end?

John Adams Rants

Complaints about the mother country were percolating among some colonists.

John Adams was one complainer, a brilliant if peppery young lawyer drawn into politics by his outrage over the Stamp Act. As he ranted, it "would drain the country of its cash, strip multitudes of all their property, and reduce them to absolute beggary." He called on the world to recognize "that we can never be slaves" and he was just about the only Founder who didn't own any slaves himself. He asked whether the colonies were to be "vassals" of Parliament or "totally independent"—clearly the latter, he answered.

These were dangerous, treasonous things for him to say.

The most enraging part of all this was that Parliament had no representatives from the colonies nor did it want any. No one in the colonies had a say in how the tax money was being spent. This was clearly a case of "taxation without representation." How was this even legal?

The colonists did agree that Parliament could make laws, but insisted that only their own elected representatives could tax them. With Britain some three thousand miles away—how could it justify Parliament having supreme authority over the colonies?

TAXES IN BRITAIN

The British were burdened with enormous taxes—yet only a small percentage of males could vote. So technically they were taxed without representation, too. They didn't really see why the Americans were making such a big deal out of getting taxed.

In Boston, the third-largest city in the colonies, some folks rioted, chanting, "Liberty, property, and *no stamps!*" Mobs threw rocks and bricks at customs officials in charge of collecting the tax. They trashed one stamp collector's house. This kind of mob action scared the daylights out of many people.

Then Britain's interference took a turn for the worse. Two days after passing the Stamp Act, Parliament passed the Quartering Act: colonies had to provide quarters (housing) and food for British troops—including candles, beer, bedding, and whatever else they needed. This intrusiveness was obnoxious, but for the moment it wasn't as pressing a matter as the tax.

Debate in Parliament raged on as the British reacted to the pressure from the colonies. The following year, in March 1766, with a little pushing from our man in London, Ben Franklin, Great Britain repealed, or took back, the Stamp Act.

Which was great news for the moment . . . except that the British had more in mind.

Tea Looms on the Horizon

Just to make it clear who was boss, Parliament promptly passed the Declaratory Act. This act affirmed its authority to pass binding laws over the colonies. The British were once again insisting that Parliament had total control over the colonies. That made it sound like they had other abusive laws up their sleeve.

This also seemed to open the door to *more* taxes, *more* ways for the British to raise money from Americans without their consent.

Sure enough, a year later came the Townshend Acts of 1767. With this new series of laws, Parliament wanted to tax all tea, paint, lead, paper, and glass brought into the colonies.

As you might expect by now, this was like poison to the colonists.

Parliament kept debating with itself and finally repealed the Townshend Acts. But it insisted on keeping one small tax on tea and increased the number of customs officials and their power to collect the money by force if necessary, like breaking into warehouses or seizing suspicious cargo off ships. It was one last arbitrary, rude gesture: they still had supreme rule over the colonies.

It turned out tea was a much bigger deal than you might think.

CHAPTER 3

A Kid Dies in Boston

Grumble, mumble, grrr.

Those were the sounds of more and more objections to the tightening grip of the British. The colonists plotted ways to avoid buying British goods—officially boycotting them. They increased smuggling. As much as 80 percent of tea, for example, was smuggled in from Holland in wine casks or under containers of other goods. They plotted rebellion. Any way to resist the British, the colonists took it.

In Massachusetts, Boston was getting a certain reputation for being the city most opposed to British rule. That was thanks to the loudest grumbler of all, a failed Bostonian businessman and agitator named Samuel Adams.

SAMUEL ADAMS

Samuel Adams was well-educated, though probably irritating with his frequent quotations from the lessons of *Aesop's Fables*. But as a student at Harvard, which ranked students by their family's social standing, he'd lost his high ranking after his father went bankrupt due to a British technicality. He was reduced to working as a waiter in the dining hall, and the humiliation left him bitter against the British. Plus, he was a rebel at heart.

As an adult, Adams was a failure at just about everything—merchant, malter (someone who produced the malt necessary for brewing beer), tax collector—except life as a political activist. At this point he didn't really have a job, so he was the patriot with the most free time to agitate, or argue and persuade, for the cause.

Suffering occasional tremors from an unknown cause, he wasn't a strong speaker in public, and his shabbiness scared people—he didn't care about appearance and wore cheap jackets and wigs. But he excelled at writing angry letters to newspapers—thousands of them under various names, to make it seem that all of Boston was outraged. He spent many evenings in taverns. A strict Puritan, he wasn't drinking so much as ranting and convincing others to join him, using his brilliance to recruit more patriots.

Samuel Adams was a political activist and able to convince
more patriots to join him.

"It does not require a majority to prevail," he said, "but rather an irate, tireless minority keen to set brush fires in people's minds." Adams excelled at setting brush fires.

Sensing the unrest in Boston, the British sent red-coated troops over in 1768 to patrol the streets and squash the resistance. Because of that dreadful Quartering Act, the soldiers had to be "quartered" in Boston's homes, housed and fed by the colonists. This was cruel and unfair, causing the whole city to teem with resentment.

The First Death

The tension was so high between the redcoats and Bostonians that violence was inevitable. In this poisonous atmosphere, children were often the ones bold enough to confront the soldiers, thinking they could get away with it. They would hurl snowballs, oyster shells, rotten eggs, and rocks at the redcoats—it was a new game to play.

Then, in one skirmish between the two groups, the redcoats shot back. In the 1770 melee, a nineteen-year-old was wounded and an eleven-year-old boy, Christopher Seider, was killed. Christopher's was technically the first death of the American Revolution. He was seen as a martyr. Child victims infuriated the patriots, and his was the largest funeral held in America at the time.

PATRIOTS AND LOYALISTS

At this point, more and more colonists were becoming patriots to the American rebel cause. But a significant minority, at least one out of five people, with strong ties to the mother country remained loyal to Great Britain and didn't want to rock the boat. Known as loyalists, this group included wealthy landowners, British government officials with important jobs they didn't want to lose, the clergy of the Church of England (Britain's national church), many in Georgia who wanted British protection against Indian attacks, and others.

As patriots grew louder and ever more dominant, loyalists had to keep lowering their profile, sometimes fleeing to England or Canada.

Family members could be on different sides of the conflict. William Franklin, the son of Ben Franklin, one of the most famous patriots of all, was a British governor of New Jersey and staunchly loyal to the Crown. William was imprisoned for three years and forced into exile. After 1775, except for one brief meeting, Ben never saw his son again: "Nothing has ever hurt me so much."

It was often hard to keep track of the two sides. This war was so confusing that it's been estimated that thousands of soldiers actually switched sides during its course—sometimes more than once.

The Massacre

A few weeks after Christopher's death came another even more appalling clash. On March 5, 1770, a wigmaker's young apprentice apparently taunted a British officer for not paying a bill. An angry crowd gathered, flustering the soldiers who were present, until finally a panicked soldier fired into the crowd, provoking chaos.

Five unarmed civilians were shot and killed. They included two seventeen-year-old apprentices and the half-Indian, half-African Crispus Attucks, a seafarer often considered the first adult martyr to die for American freedom.

One witness wept at the sight of "the blood of our fellow Citizens flowing down the gutters like water."

APPRENTICES

Some of the earliest and most fervent patriots were teenage boys learning a trade for little to no pay. Apprenticeship was a way for them to master a skill and become self-sufficient. It lasted seven years and could be grueling, with the boys living away from their families and with harsh penalties for running away. Many hated their lives and thought of joining the Revolution as a way to liberate themselves. Their idols were author Thomas Paine and scientist Ben Franklin, who were both former apprentices.

Samuel Adams pounced on the five killings as an opportunity to stir the pot. He labeled the event the Boston Massacre—"part of a settled plot to massacre the inhabitants." Technically, a massacre involves wholesale slaughter of a large unarmed group, but Adams was expertly turning the moment into propaganda for the rebel cause.

"Remember the bloody Massacre!" he urged Bostonians.

The Agitators
Samuel Adams founded the Sons of Liberty, a secret movement for American independence. It *had* to be secret—the punishment for treason, trying to overthrow the British government, was death.

The earliest meetings were supersecret, and then as the numbers grew, the rebels met in bars and public meeting halls. These were assemblies, technically illegal, for anyone who wanted to come, not just elected officials. About one-quarter of the male colonists couldn't read, nor could about half of colonial women, so these meetings were a way to keep everyone in the loop and stay on top of the quickly changing scene.

★ ★ ★ ★ ★ ★ ★ ★ ★ ★

TWO MORE AGITATORS: JOHN ADAMS AND JOHN HANCOCK

John Adams was a second cousin to Samuel Adams. Fifteen years his junior, John hadn't been particularly close with Samuel until the patriot cause united them. John was a successful lawyer who went along with Samuel's idea to represent in court the British soldiers of the Boston Massacre. They faced severe punishment on murder charges, but John argued for their freedom, saying that the real villain was Britain for sending the troops here in the first place—exactly the message Samuel wanted to send. (Most of the soldiers were acquitted, but two were convicted of manslaughter and had their hands branded.) Defending British soldiers made John unpopular in certain circles, but it also made him famous, which he liked. John, together with his wife, Abigail, had come to view the taxes as a tool of oppression, and they believed that, while Britain may have once had the colonists' best interests at heart, that was no longer the case.

Samuel Adams also had an unlikely alliance with flashy **John Hancock**, the richest man in America. Owner of a lucrative shipping business, John saw Samuel as a genius politically and began funding the Sons of Liberty. John also feared damage by patriot mobs to his mansion and other property and sensed that Samuel—the most prominent patriot—was the only one who could control a mob and keep his property safe. A strong speaker, John was popular with everyone, unusually generous to the poor, and threw great parties, with hundreds of gallons of fine wine for the crowd.

★ ★ ★ ★ ★ ★ ★ ★ ★ ★

These three patriots, working *way* behind the scenes, plotted and planned America's next moves.

They were almost ready when Parliament lobbed

the next bombshell. In May of 1773 it passed a whole act just about tea. The Tea Act kept the hated tax. But at the same time it also cut the price of tea in half.

What?

It turned out that Britain wanted Americans to buy their tea from the East India Company, a British company with huge stores of tea piling up in warehouses. Mismanaged and corrupt, the company was doing poorly and dragging the British economy down with it. Britain was desperate to save it.

Tea was imported to the colonies from the British East India Company.

In other words, Britain wanted a monopoly—no more smuggling tea from Holland or anywhere else. Americans could *only* purchase tea from the East India Company. Whatever tea the company sent had to be accepted and paid for with a deposit on the cost plus the tax.

With the British trying for a monopoly on tea, the colonists worried what *other* goods they would try to monopolize—just at the time when more and more colonists were becoming eager consumers of all kind of goods.

The patriots, men and women, sizzled with irritation.

DAUGHTERS OF LIBERTY

Some women formed Daughters of Liberty groups. They took an active role in the patriot cause by boycotting British tea and getting it from other sources, even making their own. Having tea had become an important household ritual, a civilized thing to do, with women brewing and serving it. It was an excuse to have friends over and show off all kinds of teapots and tea sets.

Having and serving tea was an important household ritual
for women in the colonies.

But it also provided a way for women to get together—they weren't supposed to be at taverns—and keep up with the latest patriot news.

Women did much else behind the scenes to help the cause. They saved linen and cotton rags to be used in making paper so newspapers could remain another source to spread the news.

More Action by Women

One of the most influential writers of the war was Mercy Otis Warren. Like most women of the day, she had no formal education. But she listened in while her brothers were being tutored for college. She wrote plays, poems, and eloquent letters. She sent letters full of anti-British, pro-liberty thoughts and advice to just about every male leader involved in the American Revolution, plus Abigail Adams and Martha Washington: "Britain, like an unnatural parent, is ready to plunge her dagger into the bosom of her affectionate offspring."

A Notable Patriot

An active Daughters of Liberty member named Esther de Berdt Reed raised a large sum of money for the American troops. She wanted to give the money directly to the soldiers, but George Washington feared they would blow it on alcohol. Instead, she spent it on having 2,200 shirts made for the men by her Ladies Association of Philadelphia. Women in other colonies followed her example and organized similar groups. Reed explained her patriotism in a printed article as a call to action—but she also wanted to prove, in this sexist era, that women were capable of publishing political opinions.

Esther de Berdt Reed was a Daughter of Liberty member and supported
the troops by raising money and making shirts for the soldiers.

About Tea, But Not About Tea

The Sons of Liberty stewed, reacting to the Tea Act with
one warning after another. Some were polite and some
were not, threatening to "exterminate such malignant
and dangerous persons"—the tax officials—or destroy
their property. At least one official was tarred and feath-
ered, an awful, though not fatal, form of punishment.

What Was the Deal with Tea?

Tea seems like a trivial thing to get riled up about.

People rarely drank water then, believing it dangerously polluted,
a custom carried over from Europe. They washed down meals with

alcohol—and, increasingly, tea. Boiling the water made it safe. Ministers urged people to drink tea instead of rum. It was healthier than alcohol, soothing and warm. At first it was a luxury item, exotic, but soon anyone could afford it. Estimates vary, but by 1769 people were drinking almost a cup of tea a day.

Some historians have speculated that the caffeine in tea was keeping the colonists more awake and stimulated, as opposed to the effects of alcohol. They were working harder than ever, and with more candles and candlesticks being imported, they could do more things at night—including plot rebellion.

★ ★ ★ ★ ★ ★ ★ ★ ★ ★

But all the fuss over tea wasn't, of course, about the actual black leaves. It was about liberty.

On October 18, 1773, Americans got word that ships full of the despised tea from the East India Company were on their way to Boston. Forty-six tons of the stuff, neatly packed into wooden chests, that had to be bought and paid for. The ships—the *Dartmouth*, the *Eleanor*, and the *Beaver*—would take a month to make the dangerous journey across the ocean and land at Griffin's Wharf.

The Sons of Liberty ramped itself into overdrive. They labeled this news "a violent attack upon the liberties of America." The meetings they organized grew so big—between five and seven thousand people attending—that they were moved from Faneuil Hall to the Old South Meeting House, the largest building in Boston.

A bloody clash seemed all but inevitable.

CHAPTER 4

Weirdest Tea Party Ever

On November 28, 1773, the first of the British ships sailed into the harbor, followed by two more.

The next twenty days in Boston were tense ones.

The patriots wanted the ships to turn around and sail right back to London. The captains refused. By British law, they couldn't return without first unloading their cargo: a total of 342 large, heavy chests of black tea.

The armed Sons of Liberty, masterminded by Samuel Adams, prevented the captains from getting that tea off the ships and onto the wharf. A guard of twenty-five men, led by a lemon importer, and later another guard of twenty-five, led by a rum distiller, went on patrol to make sure the tea stayed on board. Anyone trying to unload it, the patriots threatened, would be "considered and treated as wretches unworthy to live, and be made the first victims of our just resentment."

But *something* had to happen to that tea within eighteen days, before midnight the night of December 16. Otherwise the British customs officials could seize the tea and somehow force the colonies to pay for it.

Samuel Adams had his wildest plan yet up his sleeve.

Tea Overboard!

On the night of December 16, a loud whistle sounded, calling some hundred ordinary men from all walks of life to gather together. Mostly young, they ranged in age from teens to nine men over the age of forty. Disguising their identities was important, and many wore crude costumes meant to imitate Mohawk Indians. They marched to the wharf, boarded the ships, and ordered the captains and crews belowdecks.

Then, working as quickly as possible, they attacked the chests with axes and hatchets and hoisted them overboard. The boxes splashed, but the tea was silent: precious black tea leaves floated down the Charles River, a quiet explosion of tea.

Roughly one hundred men worked together to dump heavy chests of black tea from Britain into the river in protest.

Speed was crucial. Armed British warships were patrolling the harbor, and the tea throwers and their witnesses expected British orders to fire on them at any moment.

We imagine the night was rowdy, noisy, a free-for-all. But it was the opposite. There was no violence. No one was killed. A mostly silent crowd of at least a thousand watched in awe from the shore.

What we now call the Boston Tea Party was over in a short three hours.

Tea Partiers Anonymous

We know a few famous names, but not everyone's, as the event was veiled in secrecy. Some Sons of Liberty were there, but definitely not the most famous—Samuel Adams and John Hancock. The danger was too great for them to appear. The men swore never to reveal one anothers' names, and many kept their promise. To this day we don't know for sure who was there.

The stakes couldn't have been higher: they faced civil and criminal charges for destruction of private property. Punishment for theft in Massachusetts was hanging—a young colonist had been hanged for it just weeks earlier.

This was theft on a gigantic scale: 342 chests of tea, worth more than $1.7 million in today's money.

Not to mention that these men (and women very active behind the scenes) were technically committing treason, betraying the mother country, and could have been executed on the spot.

IGNORE THE PICTURES

No photos of the Boston Tea Party exist, of course, and any drawings of it were done many years later. They are full of inaccuracies. Sometimes a large full moon is shown, when the moon was just a thin crescent that night. Or the men are wearing elaborate Indian headdresses, when their disguises were mostly a hasty matter of blankets, faces blackened with a smear of charcoal or burnt cork, and maybe a feather from a goose quill pen. Eyewitness accounts of that night can be way off—thousands later claimed to be there who were not.

A Whole New Era

John Adams gloated in his diary: "This is the most magnificent movement of all. There is a dignity, a majesty, a sublimity, in this last [latest] effort of the patriots, that I greatly admire."

He was almost making a speech: "The people should never rise, without doing something to be remembered—something notable and striking. This destruction of the tea is so bold, so daring, so firm, intrepid and inflexible, and it must have so important consequences, and so lasting, that I can't but consider it as an epoch in history"—starting a whole new era.

John became convinced the two countries could never be reconciled.

Hancock leaped to agree: "No one circumstance could possibly have taken place more effectually to unite the colonies than this maneuver of the tea."

The Boston Tea Party was one of the most powerful political protests in history. This was no mere tea party—it had serious consequences and led directly to war.

CHAPTER 5

This Means War

John Hancock was a bit premature in claiming the colonists were united at this point. For example, most Southerners, including George Washington, didn't approve of what some were calling "the destruction of the tea" or "the affair." They thought it was vandalism, pure and simple, and they feared anarchy, the breakdown of law and order. Revolution was a scary proposition.

But in Britain, what happened that night was considered an act of war.

One British governor raged that this was "the boldest stroke that had been struck against British rule in America."

Britain's first response was to charge Samuel Adams and John Hancock with the crimes of high treason and high misdemeanors, ordering them to be brought to England to be hanged and quartered. General Thomas Gage, the commander of all British troops in North America, had been keeping the king up to speed on the most notorious rebels.

BEING QUARTERED

"While you are still living your bodies are to be taken down, your bowels torn out . . . your head then cut off, and your bodies divided each into four quarters."

Instead of giving himself up, Hancock announced that war was now desirable. He called on the people to arm themselves and get ready to "fight for their houses, land, wives, children . . . their liberty and their God" in order that "these noxious vermin will be swept forever from the streets of Boston."

Escalating Bullying

Then from Britain came punishing measures intended to force the Bostonians into obedience. These were the Intolerable (Coercive) Acts.

Intolerable was the key word. Town meetings were outlawed, and the 1691 charter of the elected ruling council of Massachusetts was revoked. Replacing it was a military government under General Gage. More troops were sent over. At Gage's headquarters in Boston, he had four regiments—perhaps four thousand men—under his command.

With the 1774 Boston Port Act, Parliament forcibly shut down the city's port. No goods could be shipped in or out. The most dire effect was that the food supplies started dwindling.

The Bullying Backfires

The British were truly acting like bullies, making Boston an example. They were gambling that the city would pay for the cost of the lost tea and show the other colonies that they had to buckle down, too.

But Boston called their bluff and did no such thing. All this punishment backfired and simply propelled the level of resentment much higher.

The Intolerable Acts were not to be tolerated. They had the effects of turning Boston into a martyr and uniting the colonies more than they ever had been before. Other colonies came to the city's defense, sending in food to make sure no one starved. Other tea parties took place up and down the coast.

From Virginia, the brilliant speaker Patrick Henry chimed in: "If our sister colony of Massachusetts Bay is enslaved we cannot long remain free. . . . UNITED WE STAND, DIVIDED WE FALL."

PATRICK HENRY

A patriot lawyer, **Patrick Henry** first gained fame while protesting the Stamp Act before the Virginia House of Burgesses in 1765. Arguing that it was only the colonial assemblies that had the right to impose taxes upon themselves, not Britain, Henry raised hackles, with some thinking his speech was treason. It might have been the most visible anti-British political action by any colonist so far.

Also from Virginia, a rising young lawyer named Thomas Jefferson ranted: "An attack made on one of our sister colonies, to compel submission to arbitrary taxes, is an attack made on all British America"—that was the way some colonists still referred to themselves.

The Tea Party was sparking something brand-new: self-respect among the colonists.

It clearly was now time to hold the first general colonial meeting ever. If the colonies could only organize together, maybe they *could* stand up to the mother country after all.

Enter the First Continental Congress. It took place from September 5 to October 26, 1774, at Carpenters' Hall in Philadelphia. It was the very first version of our present Congress and a leap toward thirteen colonies becoming one country.

The first Continental Congress took place in Philadelphia in 1774.

Committing Treason in Philadelphia

Fifty-six men made the journey from twelve colonies (Georgia, still mostly loyalist, did not participate). They included patriots like Patrick Henry, George Washington, John and Samuel Adams, and others. The delegates spoke and acted collectively for all the people of the colonies. To promote unity, delegates gave one vote to each colony regardless of its size.

In this first gathering of the colonists, the debates were long and heated. Excellent speakers put forth fiery arguments for both the patriot and the loyalist sides, showing stark disagreements.

Some still called Britain home and considered themselves part of its empire. They clung to the thought of themselves as British, demanding their rights as British citizens. Some didn't want the colonists—from such very diverse areas—to unite at all. A good many were uncomfortable, prejudiced against those from other colonies for various reasons, major and minor. Showing his snobbery, Washington disliked New Englanders—"an exceedingly dirty and nasty people," he once said (though he later changed his mind after he worked with several who impressed him). He and others despised recent immigrants, like Germans from Pennsylvania and New York, who favored independence.

Those from Pennsylvania ranted against the rebels in Massachusetts, the colony most likely to use this shocking new word *independence*. Pennsylvania was the host colony, the most influential, and the one most in favor of peacefully reconciling with Great Britain. It had sway over New York, New Jersey, Maryland, and Delaware—none of which voted for independence at this meeting.

Debates were fueled by a lot of coffee, which the colonists had turned to during the tea boycott.

Colonists turned to drinking coffee while they boycotted British tea.

The delegates were still too far apart to agree on everything, but amazingly enough, they did reach a compromise. Meeting in their secret sessions, they rejected a plan for reconciling British authority with colonial freedom.

They were now outlaws.

One Month to War

By mid-October the Congress had declared thirteen Parliament actions unconstitutional according to the British constitution (we didn't have our own yet). It also had passed resolutions defining individual rights to "life, liberty, and property." It called for a general boycott of British goods, especially tea. It pledged to stop the exporting of American goods, like tobacco and indigo, to Britain. It also denounced taxation without representation and the maintenance of the British army in the colonies without their consent. It petitioned the Crown for a redress of all the grievances accumulated since 1763.

From the Crown the colonists received only silence.

But from Philadelphia, for the first time, the colonies were speaking with a single voice.

Patrick Henry said it best: "I am not a Virginian, but an American."

Hancock gave an emotional speech and urged the formation of "the United States of America," one of the very first times this name was used.

A historic new entity was struggling to be born—at the same time that secrecy was more important than ever. Calling for rebellion against the king was still technically treason.

The group knew this struggle was far from over. Continued silence—or worse—was bound to come from the king. So the delegates' last act was to set a date for a second Congress to meet on May 10, 1775, to take further action.

But as this Congress wrapped up in October, real-life events were outpacing passionate speeches. An attack from the British seemed imminent.

Alarmed, Richard Henry Lee from Virginia proposed the founding of a national military force. Congress voted him down. They didn't have the funds, and they just weren't prepared to take this major step.

But by November 1774, a short month later, Hancock was calling for twelve thousand more men to volunteer for the militias.

CHAPTER 6

The First Shots

Outside of Congress, action—military action—was taking precedence over words. The colonies were hurtling toward war.

In March 1775, Patrick Henry gave his most famous speech, rousing colonists still uncommitted to military action—the "Liberty or Death" speech. Speaking in Richmond, he urged his fellow Virginians to mobilize troops.

"I know not what course others may take, but as for me, give me liberty or give me death!" was his thundering conclusion.

Virginia mobilized—Henry became a colonel in its army—and so did other colonies.

In April, General Gage ordered the arrest of Samuel Adams and John Hancock, architects of the Boston Tea Party and the biggest outlaws of all, with orders to shoot on sight.

Seven hundred British soldiers were on the march to the Massachusetts towns of Lexington and Concord, looking for them. They were also ordered to search for hidden military supplies rumored to be in Concord.

The Midnight Rides

The Sons of Liberty had trusty spies in place, knew about the British troops' plan, and had gotten the supplies out of Concord. Now they had to figure out how to alert the Massachusetts militia to be ready for attack.

On April 18, 1775, a Son of Liberty named Paul Revere took his famous midnight ride to warn colonists that British forces were approaching the towns of Concord and Lexington. In addition to Revere, there were two other riders, not as famous, who spread the news that night.

The American militiamen, under the leadership of Captain John Parker, waited in tension.

PAUL REVERE—IGNORE THE POEMS

Paul Revere was a prosperous and prominent Boston silversmith, just the man to see if you wanted a new silver teapot. His most famous deed, alerting the colonial militia, was memorialized in the poem "Paul Revere's Ride" by Henry Wadsworth Longfellow: "Listen, my children, and you shall hear/Of the midnight ride of Paul Revere. . . ."

But the challenge of telling true events in rhyme usually means the facts suffer. A few corrections to Longfellow's poem: Revere never actually finished his ride. He was captured by a British patrol just outside of Lexington; he was released, but they took away his horse. Revere also never shouted "The British are coming!" His mission was secret, so he wouldn't have shouted. And the colonists were themselves still technically British subjects. Rather he warned "The Regulars are out," a word meaning British soldiers.

SYBIL LUDINGTON, ANOTHER MIDNIGHT RIDER

One of the other crucial riders later in the war was a 16-year-old girl. She set off at nine o'clock one rainy night in 1777 to warn the colonists in Danbury, Connecticut, of the approach of British forces. Her father, a New York colonel named Henry Ludington, had complete trust that Sybil was brave and strong enough for the job. Defending herself when necessary, she rode until dawn. Her journey was twice that of Revere's, totaling 40 miles. Among those she warned were 400 soldiers ready to eject the enemy from the area. George Washington later commended

Sybil Ludington was one of the brave female patriots.

Sybil Ludington for heroism, but so far there are no famous poems about her.

On April 19 at four in the morning, the militiamen spotted the British a mile away. They weren't that hard to miss. Marching in formation, wearing their bright red coats, the seven hundred soldiers converged. They were so confident and cocky about conquering these unpolished American troops that they didn't anticipate injuries. They hadn't even brought a doctor along.

WHY RED?

Wouldn't the British have realized that wearing bright red coats would make them more easily targeted? Some historians have proposed that they chose red so that blood wouldn't show. The truth is that red, at the time, was cheaper and easier to produce than any other color. Dyeing fabric red could be done in one step, instead of requiring several steps as did other colors. Certainly, at some points during the war, particularly at the most chaotic moments, the red coats did work to the advantage of the Americans in making the enemy more visible.

The British uniforms and supplies were far superior to those of the colonists.

The Famous Shot

Captain Parker ordered his teenaged drummer to start beating his drum. It was a signal. Some seventy men and boys, from ages sixteen to sixty-five, began gathering at Lexington's town common.

Leaders on both sides had ordered their troops not to fire, but all was mayhem and someone did fire. It's most likely that the first shot of the American Revolution—the "shot heard round the world"—was an accident coming from a nearby tavern window.

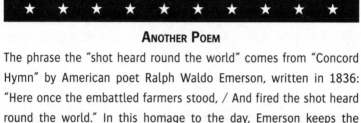

Another Poem

The phrase the "shot heard round the world" comes from "Concord Hymn" by American poet Ralph Waldo Emerson, written in 1836: "Here once the embattled farmers stood, / And fired the shot heard round the world." In this homage to the day, Emerson keeps the details vague and doesn't make mistakes with his information—except that the scene was such chaos that no one has a clue who fired the first shot that day.

Both sides promptly disobeyed their orders, and fierce fighting broke out in the start of what we now know as the Battles of Lexington and Concord.

These first shots lasted ten minutes, killing eight and wounding nine Americans, with just one British soldier wounded.

Hancock and Samuel Adams had been safely warned and were able to flee, cringing at the sound of gunshots behind them. Hancock had been in the midst of planning a delicious lunch of fresh salmon; later that day the two were lucky to be eating cold pork and potatoes.

One British major had written, predicting an easy victory after burning a few towns: "Nothing now, I am afraid, but this will ever convince these foolish bad people that England is in earnest."

The "Foolish Bad People" Beg to Differ

But instead of trouncing us, the British were forced to retreat—going backward all the way to Boston, being shot at the whole time.

Thanks to the midnight riders, the alarm surged from town to town, bringing in reinforcements. The number of militiamen rose to 3,600 from forty different towns, blitzing the retreating redcoats with heavy gunfire.

The British were disgusted—these snipers weren't even in uniform and kept appearing and disappearing into the woods—although General Gage did admit they weren't quite the "despicable rabble" he'd been expecting.

But the British had expected the colonists to flinch, and they didn't.

GUERRILLA WARFARE

Throughout the war against the well-trained British soldiers—known as the regulars because they were part of a standing, full-time army—the underequipped Americans had to go irregular. They often turned to untraditional tactics—guerrilla warfare, which means using improvised means not found in military textbooks.

Guerrillas fought not in an orderly, symmetric fashion but in an asymmetric way, catching the enemy off guard. Techniques included raids, ambushes, using small groups of fighters, participation by local civilians, trickery, and more while trying to exhaust the opponents. Guerrilla warfare often worked well for the colonists, who knew the terrain much better than the British and had the advantage of mobility to attack and then dash back into forests or swamps.

The number of militiamen kept growing, far outnumbering the British soldiers. Had there been one American commander in charge overall that day, the militias might have put a quick end to the war on the spot.

PATRIOTS' DAY

With both Lexington and Concord claiming credit for firing the "shot heard round the world" and wanting a holiday to celebrate it, a compromise was reached: Patriots' Day. This holiday, celebrating the Battles of Lexington and Concord, takes place in several states, most notably in Massachusetts, where it falls on the third Monday in April. All sorts of commemorations are scheduled, most famously the annual Boston Marathon, honoring the American struggle for liberty and attracting thousands of runners from all over the world.

The Boston Marathon is one of the best-known races.
with competitors from around the world entering each year.

Shock All Around

By the end of that day's battle, the Americans had won. Seventy-three British soldiers lay dead, with hundreds wounded, versus fifty Americans killed and fifty wounded. Bostonians were stunned to see British survivors limping back into town.

No one had expected such a deadly battle that day—that soldiers on both sides would shoot to kill.

Everyone was in shock, including John Adams, who witnessed the carnage: "When I reflect and consider that the fight was between those whose parents but a few generations ago were brothers, I shudder at the thought, and there's no knowing where our calamities will end."

All around New England, more and more militiamen seized their guns and sped toward Boston. The number had reached twenty thousand by the end of April—effectively trapping the British there.

These men represented the birth of the American army, a national army even if a leaderless one.

News Traveling Slowly

Remember that there were no cell phones or even regular phones at that time. George Washington did not learn about Lexington and Concord for seven days, when the news finally reached him at his Mount Vernon estate in Virginia. King George III did not learn the news until May 28.

Boys from the Green Mountains

With those British forces now trapped in Boston and no one leader in charge of the American troops, rebels acted rather randomly—in true guerrilla fashion.

Enter an interesting character named Ethan Allen—a strong man, outlaw, huge (he was six foot six), and rabidly patriotic. Also persuasive, as he gathered patriot farmers from the Green Mountains, an area between New York and New Hampshire that was so independent it wasn't even part of a colony yet. These eighty men were the Green Mountain Boys.

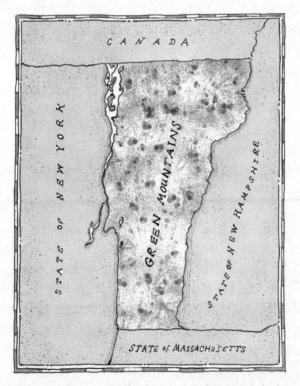

The Green Mountains were outside of any colony but provided a base for rebel soldiers to plan guerrilla attacks on the British.

On May 10, with information he got from a spy, Allen and his Boys went into action. Silently they rowed across Lake Champlain to Fort Ticonderoga, a strategic British fort in northern New York.

They arrived at the fort just before sunrise. The soldier supposedly guarding it was asleep. Eighty yelling men pounced on him, and he jolted awake and ran into the fort . . . followed by the Boys.

Allen charged into the commander's bedroom and, with his sword raised, demanded an immediate surrender. The commander, minus his pants, had no choice.

So, in his sneak attack, Allen was able to seize Fort Ticonderoga. The best part of the day was their capture of a hundred British cannons, which were desperately needed by American soldiers.

But also the ambush was crucial to morale: it proved that the British could be outsmarted.

Back in Boston

Meanwhile, the British were trying to escape their trap in Boston. They tried to take control of two hills above it—Breed's Hill and Bunker Hill. But patriot spies in Boston did their job, and colonists beat the British to those locations and were able to build a fort.

The next battle erupted on June 17—known as the Battle of Bunker Hill (even though Breed's Hill was the main place of combat). Under the command of William Howe, the British assaulted the American fort with 2,300 troops.

Colonel William Prescott, the American commander, was all too aware of how short of ammunition his 1,200 men were. In a famous line he ordered them to make every shot count: "Don't fire till you see the whites of their eyes."

Luckily, the redcoats were marching in tidy rows that made them easy targets. Howe's men encountered devastating fire.

The British had to mount three attacks before they eventually did clear the hill—but at a serious cost. They lost more than 40 percent of their forces—with a thousand soldiers shot, and two hundred killed. Howe went on to become the British commander in chief, replacing General Gage.

The Americans lost the Battle of Bunker Hill, but still it gave them confidence. Colonial militias *could* stand up to the mighty British army.

Now it was every colonist for himself—complete chaos. The Americans needed an organized army and quick. And to make this work, the troops were going to need a leader, a really good one.

CHAPTER 7

Head and Shoulders Above the Rest

Events could hardly keep up with one another.

War had already erupted by the time the Second Continental Congress met, as planned, on May 10, 1776, in Philadelphia. This Congress became the provisional, or temporary, government of the thirteen colonies—issuing and borrowing money, establishing a postal service, and trying to manage the war even as it was already in progress.

Great Britain had an almost unsurpassable advantage here, with a long-established government in place to deal with war.

To the men in Philadelphia's State House, the deaths at Lexington and Concord were appalling: the king's men killing His Majesty's own subjects. Some wanted mere separation, others a revolution.

New members of the Second Congress included Virginia's Thomas Jefferson, the youngest at thirty-two. Benjamin Franklin, the eldest in the group at sixty-nine, was back from his years in London, and by this time totally agreed with the Adams cousins that a complete break from Great Britain was the right thing to do.

Congress declared on May 10 that the authority of the king ought to be "totally suppressed," advising all the colonies to establish governments of their own choice.

It also set about creating a navy and turning New England's militiamen into America's army, known as the Continental Army. Local militias would still help out, but the military moves of the thirteen colonies could now be coordinated.

Wanted: A Leader

The next job was to choose a leader for the new army. John Hancock was puffed with pride, having done so much for the colonies that he was counting on being offered the job.

But the two Adams cousins preferred Virginia's George Washington. He had fought in his militia and was from the biggest of the southern colonies, which would help keep them all united. He was also just plain charismatic, a natural-born leader.

Washington, normally composed, was a little rattled that day. He ran out of the room while the others debated—but he had also shown up wearing his full-dress military outfit.

The Adams cousins were very persuasive. They won, much to Hancock's disappointment, though he didn't pout for long.

On June 15, upon being appointed commander in chief, George Washington was nervous. He wrote to his wife, Martha, that the whole thing filled him with "inexpressible concern."

But he also immediately packed and left for Boston.

GEORGE WASHINGTON

George Washington was well on his way to becoming a hero. Only 43 years old at the time, he'd been working hard since his teens, never shirking his responsibilities.

As a military leader he had some experience, but not a lot. In the French and Indian War he had volunteered in a local British regiment and fought bravely if not always particularly successfully. He never led an army of more than a thousand men but was able to closely observe British military methods and strategy. After the war he'd been elected to Virginia's ruling body, the House of Burgesses.

George Washington was a natural-born leader, and he inspired others to join the patriot cause.

He was known for having no fear, extraordinary strength, and amazing survival skills. Some of his feats sound impossible, like walking untouched through gunfire. "I heard the bullets whistle, and, believe me, there is something charming in the sound," he once wrote.

Personally he was cool, calm, and collected—in fact a little wooden in his formality. He was not usually emotional, not big on touching.

He was the country's first millionaire—mainly because he married Martha, who had inherited a vast estate from her late husband, which by law went to her next husband. He was the proud owner of Mount Vernon, one of Virginia's premiere estates.

And he was really tall, easy to spot in a room, head and shoulders above other men.

Washington's acceptance of the job inspired others still on the fence to support the patriot cause. This war was such an insane gamble. But if Washington, of all people, with his money and stature, was willing to risk everything, they could, too.

WASHINGTON MYTHS

It's not true that as a boy he chopped down a cherry tree and confessed "I cannot tell a lie." The fake story was included in a children's book intended to teach lessons.

Nor is it true about his teeth being made of wood. True, he lost almost all his teeth—and further demonstrating his stamina, lost them by crude methods (think: a pair of pliers, no anesthetic).

But his false teeth were made of other teeth—human and animal. He seldom smiled, partly not wanting to reveal his fake teeth, but also life was serious. He might have paid more attention to his beloved horses' teeth—every morning he had his grooms brush them—than his own.

George Washington did have false teeth, but they were not made of wood, as many people believe.

Washington Tries to Take Control

On July 3, General Washington assumed command of his new army, the hastily assembled group of men still gathered outside Boston.

He plunged into a nightmare. The camp was filthy, with a vile smell and disorderly men and boys. He began issuing orders, starting with basics, like telling his men not to use the trenches dug for warfare as toilets.

NO NUDITY, PLEASE

"The General does not mean to discourage the practice of bathing whilst the weather is warm enough to continue it, but he expressly forbids, any persons doing it, at or near the bridge in Cambridge, where it has been observed and complained of, that many men, lost to all sense of decency

and common modesty, are running about naked upon the bridge, whilst passengers, and even ladies of the first fashion in the neighborhood, are passing over it, as if they meant to glory in their shame."

—General Washington

Discipline was so minimal that he even had to stop those within his own army from fighting one another. That winter a snowball fight between Massachusetts men and Virginians turned into a fistfight drawing in one thousand men. Washington dived in himself and broke up the melee.

The infighting was an annoying hindrance. "Nothing gives me more pain," he wrote, "than the frequency of complaints that are made and difference of various kinds that happen among a set of men embarked in the same great cause." How was he ever going to get these men to unite as a team?

STOP GAMBLING AND WORK OUT

"The Commander in Chief, in the most pointed and explicit terms, forbids ALL officers and soldiers playing at cards, dice, or at any games, except those of EXERCISE."

—General Washington

The prickliness among men mirrored the prickliness between the warring countries. On July 5,

Congress offered a symbolic olive branch toward Britain. It approved the Olive Branch Petition, one last-ditch attempt to avoid war. It claimed loyalty to the king and asked him to avoid further clashes.

The king wouldn't even read the petition. Instead, he was ordering the largest military deployment in Great Britain's history to assemble on America's coast, ready to attack.

The mobilization of large armed forces, together with the lack of a gesture toward conciliation, convinced many colonists who were still torn. Some still believed the Americans were struggling for their rights within the British Empire. But the majority of Americans increasingly came to believe that they had to secure their rights *outside* the empire.

It was becoming clearer and clearer that they had more in common with one another than with the British.

Escalation
During 1775, skirmishes took place in several places in South Carolina, Virginia, and in Montreal and Quebec in Canada.

WHY DIDN'T CANADA HELP?
What about our neighbors to the north? Canada was made up of British and French colonies, too. Couldn't they have united with us?

Given that half the population of Nova Scotia was New Englanders, they might have supported the American rebels. Some did head south to fight, but in the end Nova Scotia's isolation and its large British military presence kept it loyal to the Crown.

The French Canadians of Quebec could have jumped at the chance of getting back at their British rulers. But Parliament's Quebec Act of 1774 had guaranteed them their language, the right to practice Roman Catholicism, and French civil law. This angered the rebels, who denounced the Act and its provisions. For the French Canadians, it was largely a case of "better the devil you know than the devil you don't know," and the majority stayed out of the conflict altogether.

The losses and terror that came from the unofficial war greatly widened the breach between the colonies and the mother country. Meanwhile, Congress was gradually cutting tie after tie with Britain until separation was all but complete.

But the colonists still needed something to give a purpose to the war already started. Something bold, an official document, a statement . . . a Declaration.

Abigail Adams was among those pushing for it: "I long to hear that you have declared an independency," she wrote to her husband, John.

"Be patient," he wrote back.

Many colonists—male and female—were eager for an official declaration of independence.

ABIGAIL ADAMS

Abigail Adams, a true-blue patriot, boycotted British tea and made her own dresses or wore old ones instead of buying British fabric. But she is best remembered for the letters she wrote to her husband during the Continental Congress.

On top of all her responsibilities—running the family farm, home-schooling their children—she found time to write John letters, as many as three a day, about what was going on in the Massachusetts colony, the immorality of slavery, the necessity of breaking free of Great Britain, and what he should be accomplishing in the jobs that were taking him away from her. John typically used her opinions to help shape his own. This was a time when women didn't write for publication, but nothing stopped her from writing letters, and she felt enormously proud to be playing this role in history.

Abigail Adams wrote many letters to her husband in which she expressed her views on such important topics as independence and slavery.

CHAPTER 8

*Thinking Big: the Declaration
of Independence*

At this point, even in the midst of war, the three million colonists were *still* not all convinced that war was necessary. No one had a clue how this would end. But from all signs so far, a war would end very badly for them.

Then, in January 1776, Thomas Paine published his earthshaking pamphlet *Common Sense*.

"These are the times that try men's souls," he began. In plain but stirring language he made the case for independence. Paine believed that all humans are equal. Therefore, he argued, a government that values a monarch above everyone else is not a valid government. All kings are tyrants, not just King George III. Kings had to go.

★ ★ ★ ★ ★ ★ ★ ★ ★ ★

THOMAS PAINE

The British political activist **Thomas Paine** was brand-new in America, arriving in 1774 with the help of Ben Franklin. Seriously ill with typhoid, he had to be wrapped in a blanket and carried ashore, where Franklin's doctor awaited him.

Paine was Bohemian, living and thinking outside the limits of conventional society. He was known as "Mad Tom" to

Thomas Paine introduced radical new ideas to the young colonies.

those who found his ideas too radical, too much. He loved his new country but attacked its system of slavery and its treatment of Indians. He envisioned America as a potential utopia: "Not a place upon earth might be so happy as America."

His pamphlet turned into an all-time bestseller, selling 150,000 copies in its first six months. Paine donated his profits to buy gloves for the American troops.

Paine Works a Powerful Change

A passionate argument for starting a new country, *Common Sense* had an explosive impact, persuading those still undecided. America didn't *need* Britain—it had created itself with its own hard work. According to Paine, it made no sense for America to be ruled by a government so far away.

For the young colonies, the written word was an important part of their fight for independence from Great Britain.

John Adams thought Paine went too far and called his pamphlet "a poor, ignorant, malicious, short-sighted, crapulous mass."

But more people agreed with Washington, who wrote, "I find *Common Sense* is working a powerful change . . . in the minds of many men."

And Adams did come around: "Without the pen of the author of *Common Sense*, the sword of Washington would have been raised in vain," he finally admitted.

It was Paine, this brand-new immigrant to America, who turned the tide. He made it okay to talk about this taboo, only-whispered-about subject of independence in public.

Back in Boston

In early March, General Howe, in charge of the British still in Boston, looked up to see some sixty cannons on the hillside pointed right at him.

Remember the cannons stolen by Ethan Allen in his daring sneak attack at dawn (see page 74)? Washington had ordered them to be hauled across the mountains on sleds and secretly put into position to fire.

It turned out to be a savvy plan. On March 17, 1776, the British were forced to evacuate Boston—and they never returned. That was the good news.

The bad news was that the British government, in one of its traditional moves, purchased some thirty thousand troops from various German princes and sent them to fight America. These were paid soldiers—mercenaries—working for money and not out of loyalty to a country.

Colonists saw this as a serious violation of the rules of war. Few acts by the Crown roused so much antagonism in America as the use of foreign mercenaries. This violation was a factor in getting Massachusetts and Pennsylvania to finally agree on independence.

The Crucial Lee Resolution

At the Second Continental Congress in Philadelphia, Richard Henry Lee of Virginia proposed independence on June 7, 1776: "That these united colonies are, and of right ought to be, free and independent states." Lee was a good speaker, gesturing with a hand wrapped in black silk, having lost his fingers in a hunting accident.

Now the delegates had to vote yea or nay. The vote on the Lee Resolution was crucial—it had to be unanimous. Unless all voted yes, it was meaningless and could very well be a prediction for a civil war among the colonies in the future.

Within days, 132 British ships amassed offshore. The largest fleet ever assembled was on its way to New York, the second largest city in the colonies.

It was an appropriate time to be twitchy. The country was already at war, which, if lost, would result in the capture of everyone in Congress.

FOUNDING FATHERS?

People love to praise the Founding Fathers—usually including Washington, John Adams, Jefferson, James Madison, and Alexander Hamilton. But recently historians have been using other terms. Opinions vary, but most want to broaden the term to Founders—to honor women and all the brave, treasonous, not-necessarily-famous rebels who started this country, not just a few elite men.

Many brave men and women contributed to the founding
of our country—more than just the notable names we know.

★ ★ ★ ★ ★ ★ ★ ★ ★ ★ ★

Enter Thomas Jefferson

On June 11, the Committee of Five took shape. Thomas Jefferson, John Adams, Benjamin Franklin, Roger Sherman, and Robert R. Livingston were chosen to prepare a statement backing up the decision to declare independence.

Their mission was to justify the break to the world, to make our wobbly "country" appear stable. We clearly needed military help, and to secure as much aid as possible, it was crucial to make a grand statement about who we were.

ROGER SHERMAN AND ROBERT L. LIVINGSTON

Three of the Committee of Five were already well-known. Another was Roger Sherman, an influential lawyer and politician from Connecticut. He's not as famous as the others because he wasn't the best speaker. But Jefferson called him "a man who never said a foolish thing in his life," and John Adams hailed him as "one of the soundest and strongest pillars of the Revolution."

Robert R. Livingston was also an established lawyer and was deeply involved in governing New York. But he had no input on the draft of the Declaration and in fact never signed it.

Among these five fine minds, no one took notes. So we don't know a lot of detail about who decided what. We know John Adams declined to write the statement himself, admitting, "I am obnoxious, suspected, and unpopular"—all basically true. He delegated the job of drafting the Declaration to the more popular Jefferson.

THOMAS JEFFERSON

Young as he was, **Thomas Jefferson** was a successful lawyer already famous for his writing skills. "Nothing is more important than to acquire a facility of developing our ideas on paper," he believed.

Besides public service, his life's work was designing his pride and joy, his mountaintop estate at Monticello, where he was economically dependent on his 120 slaves. He threw gourmet dinner parties with shockingly expensive wines, invented labor-saving devices, played violin for as many as three hours a day, and championed animal rights.

As probably the most well-read person in America, he was a notorious book hoarder, amassing some 10,000 titles. One was an English translation of the Koran, the sacred text of Islam, which he bought as a law student. A staunch defender of religious liberty—the separation of church and state—he was tolerant of all religions (though he belonged to no church himself). Later, campaigning for religious freedom in Virginia, Jefferson followed John Locke, his idol, in demanding recognition of the religious rights of Muslims, Jews, Hindus, and even atheists.

Thomas Jefferson was a talented young lawyer whose
passionate ideas influenced the new country.

Eighteen Days with Thomas Jefferson
Jefferson left Congress to hole himself up in a small, airless rented room, hunched over his portable mahogany

writing desk. He would rise at dawn, soak his feet in a bucket of cold water, play violin for a while, drink some tea, then get out his quill pen, honing every word, every sentence, every punctuation mark.

At last, after eighteen long days, he emerged on June 28 with his one-page draft of the Declaration of Independence.

Jefferson's goal was to write a public statement capturing the "American mind." So he used grand language meant for a world stage: "We hold these truths to be sacred and undeniable," he wrote, "that all men are created equal; that from that equal creation they derive in rights inherent and inalienable, among which are are the preservation of life, liberty, and the pursuit of happiness."

Among other goals, Jefferson wanted to send a message to a worldwide audience: our war was not trivial, a mere dispute between colonists and rulers. It was much bigger than that, with important things to say about the rights of men. He was reaching out to potential allies, like the French, to help us with our noble cause, and he used language that would attract them, not portray our conflict as petty.

Claiming that Parliament never truly possessed sovereignty over the colonies, the Declaration went on to say that King George III, with the support of a "pretended" legislature, had persistently violated the agreement between himself as governor and the Americans as the governed. A long list of accusations was offered toward proving the point—starting with the Proclamation of 1763. With the British seeming to side with Indians over white men, Jefferson attacked King George for backing "merciless Indian Savages."

Jefferson used the Declaration to accuse King George III
of restricting the colonists' rights.

On the other hand, Jefferson included a paragraph
denouncing the African slave trade. Though dependent
on slaves himself, he blamed the king for imposing
the system in the first place: "He has waged cruel war
against human nature itself, violating its most sacred
rights . . . in the persons of a distant people who never
offended him, captivating and carrying them into

slavery in another hemisphere, or to incur miserable death in their transportation thither."

THE DECLARATION'S TWO MAIN POINTS

1. A government's main job is to protect people's rights.
2. When it does not do so, the people have the right to replace it with a new government.

In essence the document served to make the point that the people have basic rights that no ruler could take away. Rulers have the right to govern as long as the people give them the power. When the people choose to take that power away, they can do so.

These were all very startling things to say at the time. Jefferson was taking a huge personal risk with this document.

Ideas from Around the World

Besides using his own experiences as a lawyer, Jefferson brilliantly brought together the ideas of others.

He borrowed ideas from ancient Greece and Rome, as well as from George Mason, a friend and neighbor of George Washington. Mason was the main author of a Declaration of Rights and the ideas in Virginia's new constitution: "We came equals into this world, and equals shall we go out of it. All men are by nature born equally free and independent." (Mason would likely have been in Congress then but was busy being a single parent to his nine children.)

Jefferson was influenced by his favorite English philosopher, John Locke, a towering figure in the Age of Enlightenment. This was a movement that pushed Europe into using science and reason to solve problems. "Just governments are founded on consent," wrote Locke, "and are designed solely to protect the people in their inherent rights to life, liberty, and property." In other words, people had natural rights.

BEN FRANKLIN AND THE INFLUENCE OF INDIANS

As early as 1754, with the Albany Plan of Union, Benjamin Franklin had been the first colonist to propose a single government for the colonies. His first diplomatic job was as Pennsylvania's Indian commissioner, and he admired the Iroquois Confederacy uniting the Oneida, Mohawk, Cayuga, Seneca, Onondaga, and Tuscarora. The Confederacy joined six self-ruled nations in a democracy based on laws in common.

Most notably, it had a centuries-old constitution known as the Great Law of Peace, handed down through generations. Peace was not based on force of arms but on harmony over mutual goals. It always struck Franklin as a model for what the colonies could do—if what he called "six nations of ignorant savages" could do it, so could thirteen colonies. (A man of his time, he alternated between respect for Indians and dismissal of them.)

Now, as Congress debated the Declaration, they invited some 20 Iroquois Confederacy chiefs to act as advisers.

On June 28, Jefferson presented his draft. It was a hot and muggy June day, but there was another reason he was sweating.

CHAPTER 9

We Have a Declaration

Jefferson was about to endure more torture. Over the next three days, Congress pored over his work, crafting changes to his perfect prose while he tried not to scream.

Testy Congressmen debated his work twelve hours a day. Some changes were petty—from "inalienable" to "unalienable," from "neglected utterly" to "utterly neglected." They fiddled with his wording in various places: "All men are created equal, that they are endowed by their Creator with certain inalienable rights, that among these are life, liberty, and the pursuit of happiness."

Some were more substantial. The men expanded the list of charges against the king. They deleted a condemnation of the British people plus a reference to "Scotch and foreign mercenaries" (there were Scots in Congress), as well as a statement that the colonies had established themselves with no help from Britain.

Franklin Calms Jefferson

During the debates, Franklin sat next to Jefferson and tried to distract him with funny stories—though even he had a change of his own to make. He altered "we hold these truths to be sacred and undeniable" to "we hold these truths to be self-evident." Ever the scientist, Franklin wanted to move the Declaration away from religion to nature's laws.

They also took out Jefferson's denunciation of the African slave trade. It was offensive to some delegates—Georgia and South Carolina wouldn't sign a Declaration if it had an antislavery clause. So they decided to shelve this topic for the time. ("For the time" was going to mean for eighty-five years, when the Civil War broke out.)

EXCLUSIONS

In deliberately excluding African Americans and Indians, the Declaration was a contradiction to American ideals right from the start. It reflected the racism embedded in our society.

The Declaration held contradictions from the beginning. stating that all men are created equal but leaving out women. African Americans. and Indians.

It also left out women. Abigail Adams had just written a helpful reminder to her husband, John: "I desire you would remember the ladies." In that sexist, unenlightened era, women had no voice in government, and John's response was typical: "I cannot but laugh."

The All-Important Vote

The pressure was on as the delegates rushed to a last-minute vote on the Lee Resolution. As of July 1, only nine colonies were voting yes. It was a scary moment. The vote *had* to be unanimous.

The vote was postponed till the next day. By then three colonies changed sides—South Carolina, Delaware, and Pennsylvania came on board. New York was still holding out, but Congress decided to declare the vote unanimous anyway.

On July 2, 1776, with New York abstaining, the Congress "unanimously" resolved that "these United Colonies are, and of right ought to be, free and independent States."

One day later, 110 British ships were landing in New Jersey and 53 in South Carolina.

Two days later, on July 4, 1776, Congress solemnly approved the Declaration of Independence. Church bells chimed at what later became known as Independence Hall and all over Philadelphia. Patriots tore the king's coat of arms from the Philadelphia State House and later burned it in a bonfire.

Getting the Word Out

On July 5, copies of the Declaration began to be distributed, a process that would take weeks to reach all the colonies.

On July 8 came the first public reading at Independence Hall in Philadelphia. Crowds chanted, "God bless the free states of North America!"

On July 9, the Declaration was read aloud in front of New York's City Hall. Soldiers and citizens rioted, pulling down the statue of King George III and later melting it into much-needed bullets.

On July 12, British peace commissioners showed up on Staten Island, ready to accept America's submission and perhaps do some negotiation to avoid bloodshed.

But it was too late.

In Congress, New York finally fell into line on July 19.

A clerk began hand-lettering the Declaration on a large piece of parchment. He finished on August 2, titling it "The Unanimous Declaration of the Thirteen United States of America," labeled "In Congress, July 4, 1776."

The United States. Now that had a satisfying ring to it.

The Declaration was approved in Congress on July 4, 1776.

It took a month after approving the Declaration for the delegates to get around to signing it—and some never did. Why? Signers knew they were still committing treason and could be hanged for it.

Too Hot to Handle

Printers in Philly were too nervous to print the Declaration for the same reason some were afraid to sign it—fear of treason.

A printer named Mary Katherine Goddard, publisher and owner of the *Maryland Journal*, printed the first copies signed with all the names. Goddard was so brave that she put her full name on the publication—known as the *Goddard Broadside*. It was the first time the public learned who had signed the Declaration.

John Hancock was the first, inking his name with a large flourish. John Adams worked overtime to persuade the others to join Hancock. Adams wrote joyfully: "We are in the very midst of a revolution, the most complete, unexpected, and remarkable of any in the history of nations."

Sam Adams, working feverishly behind the scenes, exulted: "The Congress has at length declared the colonies free and independent states." He had accomplished his life's mission.

London had copies by August, and the document was quickly printed up in various European countries.

★ ★ ★ ★ ★ ★ ★ ★ ★ ★ ★ ★ ★

WISE WORDS

"We're not done perfecting our union, or living up to our founding creed that all of us are created equal; all of us are free in the eyes of God. . . . Our power comes from those immortal declarations first put to paper right here in Philadelphia all those years ago: We hold these truths to be self-evident, that all men are created equal; that We the People, can form a more perfect union."

—President Barack Obama, 2016

★ ★ ★ ★ ★ ★ ★ ★ ★ ★ ★ ★ ★

What Happened to the Signers?

The fifty-six signers ranged in age from twenty-six to seventy. Many of the signers survived the war and went on to political careers—as presidents, senators, governors, Supreme Court justices.

But the danger of signing was real, with awful consequences for others. New York delegate Francis Lewis's house was destroyed by the British and his wife, Elizabeth, taken prisoner; she died in jail. New Jersey's John Hart also lost his home and went into hiding, where he died.

Another New Jersey delegate, Richard Stockton, was captured and thrown in jail; during his months of harsh treatment, he recanted his signature and swore allegiance to the Crown. Virginia delegate Carter Braxton lost all his ships to the British navy and died broke.

More Paperwork

After settling on the Declaration, Congress kept going with the mammoth task of trying to get the new states working together, making the government official. They started knocking out the Articles of Confederation. These gave Congress a wide assortment of powers—waging war, controlling Indian affairs, borrowing money, and more.

The Articles had many weaknesses, but compiling them was a good exercise in preparing a written document that would guide a self-governing country. (One without kings.)

Documents to Come

The Articles of Confederation had to be ratified, or approved, by all the states, which didn't happen until 1781. This represented the birth of our national, or federal, government, and paved the way for the Constitutional Convention in 1787. *That* meeting created our for-real Constitution (1789) and our present form of a government in three parts (executive, legislative, and judicial), with the Bill of Rights for extra protection added in 1791. With the Bill of Rights, we got a guarantee that the Constitution could be changed, or amended, as necessary.

We still needed more documents to spell out *how* the goals of the Declaration would be carried out.

WISE WORDS

"Laws and institutions must go hand in hand with the progress of the human mind. As that becomes more developed, more enlightened, as new discoveries are made, new truths discovered and manners and opinions change, with the change of circumstances, institutions must advance also to keep pace with the times. We might as well require a man to wear still the coat which fitted him when a boy as civilized society to remain ever under the regimen of their barbarous ancestors."

—Thomas Jefferson

We had no flag, no constitution, no national leader, not much of an army, barely a navy.

But we did have a Declaration.

For now, it changed the Revolution, giving it a focus, and changing hesitant minds. Now the struggle became a war for an idea.

A FRIENDLY REMINDER

The Declaration and the Constitution are two different documents. Even people running for president have been known to mix them up.

The Declaration begins "When in the Course of human events," was written in 1776, and declared our goals.

The Constitution was ratified in 1789, begins with "We the People," and spelled out how the government was to operate.

No Rest for Washington

Still Washington worried: "The eyes of all our country-men are now upon us."

He could feel the weight of the world on his shoulders: "The fate of unborn millions will now depend, under God, on the current and conduct of this army.... We have, therefore, to resolve to conquer or die."

CHAPTER 10

Back to the War, and It's Not Looking Good

The Declaration was nice, but at the time it was merely a piece of paper.

In the real world, out on the battlefield, things were still grim. The odds were so much against the colonists that Washington had to come up with a strategy that sounds weird: win the war by not losing it.

His aim was for his Continental Army to simply hold on. Either the British would give up, or another country would step in to help. Until then he had to lead the army to fight defensively, not necessarily winning all the battles.

How? He was going to have to think outside the box, using the guerrilla, nontraditional ways of fighting: ambush, hit-and-run raids, spies, the element of surprise, luck. He was also going to rely on patriotism to motivate his troops into battling the odds and sticking it out.

Even this seemed impossible. As of August 1776, the army had nineteen thousand inexperienced soldiers, while Britain had thirty-two thousand trained troops plus eight thousand very tough German mercenaries.

August and September, the two months following our brave Declaration, were disastrous.

In the first major battle after the Declaration—and the largest battle of the whole war—the colonists took a serious hit. The Battle of Brooklyn (later known as the Battle of Long Island) lasted a week. More than a thousand American men were killed, wounded, or captured by General Howe's men. The slaughter was so relentless that Washington was forced to keep retreating—yes, going backward—until he was at the edge of the East River.

During the night of August 29, he was able to save his surviving troops. He rounded up all the boats within twenty miles. All night a group of Massachusetts fishermen rowed boats full of American soldiers across the river and into Manhattan. Thanks to a heavy fog at sunrise, they escaped without the British noticing.

Washington Has a Bad Day

Alas, Howe kept up the bombardment. By September 15, the British had occupied Manhattan, which was not skyscrapers then but mostly forest. Americans again were forced to retreat in disarray. This time, they were not following orders, just running for their lives.

Washington, in a rare show of fury, screamed at his retreating soldiers, physically trying to halt them. Some men just kept running—actually deserting, sometimes whole regiments at a time.

Someone overheard Washington yell, "Are these the men with whom I am to defend America?" (Even when under extreme stress, he spoke grammatically.)

Though losing control of Boston earlier that year, the British had now taken control of New York City, which was of great strategic importance. They were able to use it as a major base of operations for the rest of the war.

Washington came close to getting captured himself, until officers yanked him off the battlefield.

Don't Make Washington Mad

The following day, British buglers taunted Washington by sounding the fox-hunting call "gone away," meaning that a fox is in full flight. This was supposed to fool Washington, an avid foxhunter, into thinking that his enemies were also in flight—he could relax. But Washington found the taunt so irritating that he ordered his men to stand their ground and slowly push British troops back. The enemy was forced to withdraw.

Finally, at this, the Battle of Harlem Heights, Washington had his first victory on the battlefield. Morale went way up.

The number of his troops was going to vary, depending on whether his side seemed to be winning or losing. At any given time the American forces seldom numbered over twenty thousand. Many fell prey to disease. For each soldier killed in combat, nine died of disease, mostly due to a lack of sanitation.

After a victory, patriotism would drive more men to join the army. So would other events. In 1777, a woman from a New York patriot family, Jane McCrea, was murdered. Indians commissioned by British General John Burgoyne were blamed. The murder outraged patriots and led to a huge surge of recruiting in New York.

The more victories Washington and his army won, the more volunteers would line up to join the cause.

But after defeats, men would desert. All throughout the war Washington faced the serious and basic problem of desertion. Men would simply take off to visit families, help with harvest back on their farms, or any reason. Most were not used to being told what to do, and they didn't like it. The wretched and uncertain pay didn't help. The terms of Continental Army service were gradually increased from one to three years, and not even bounties and the offer of land kept the army up to a decent strength.

On top of everything else, Washington had to deal with troops who rebelled against *him*—the occasional mutiny. The punishment for mutiny was execution, and he resorted to it when he had to.

Who Were the Men of the Continental Army?

The troops in the Continental Army were mostly young, between the ages of fifteen and thirty. The army wasn't supposed to take boys younger than fifteen, but as the war dragged on, it wasn't so picky.

Those who served came from all walks of life, with the majority being farmers and skilled artisans. Some were drifters, but most were solid citizens with trades.

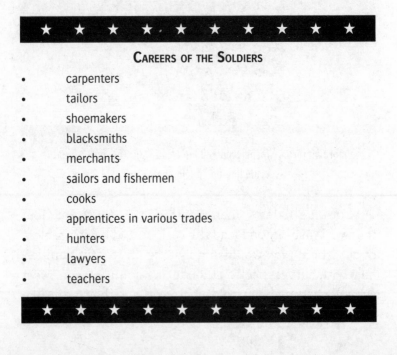

CAREERS OF THE SOLDIERS

- carpenters
- tailors
- shoemakers
- blacksmiths
- merchants
- sailors and fishermen
- cooks
- apprentices in various trades
- hunters
- lawyers
- teachers

Some were missing fingers or teeth or bore smallpox scars, proof that life in the colonies could be harsh. Almost everyone had seen someone die.

For most, it was their first experience of working with a diverse group, and they were awkward at it. Some made friends, some didn't. Manners weren't a priority for many, causing lots of childish bickering and brawls.

Washington tried to keep his men fed. But food rations could be highly irregular, depending on the weather, road conditions, and the season. On a good day, the soldiers were supposed to receive a hunk of beef, fish, or pork—including not only the meat, but bone, fat, and gristle. They got a ration of bread, baked daily inside the camp, or flour. They also got a quarter of a pint of whiskey or rum.

FIRECAKES

If the men received flour instead of bread, they made firecakes. Soldiers heated a flat rock, then mixed the flour with water, meat, and gristle, and poured the mixture on the heated rock, then flipped it over to cook the other side—like pancakes.

When properly supplied, the typical soldier carried forty-five pounds of gear—weapons, knapsack, supplies for eating, perhaps an extra blanket or shirt, and paper and pen for those who wanted to write home. There was no such thing as pajamas—men wore the same clothes day and night.

But supply problems constantly plagued the army,

and often men had to make do with whatever arms and equipment they could grab from home.

Meanwhile, on the Other Side

By contrast, the British army was a reliable, steady force of professionals. Unlike the Continental Army, they had the benefit of an actual government in place to manage the war effort and their soldiers, including decent sanitation for them.

They were an average of five years older than American men and mostly English, Scottish, and Irish, with some from Europe. Many had been farm boys, some were previously unemployed men from city slums, and others joined the army to escape fines or imprisonment. The great majority became efficient soldiers as a result of training and discipline. The officers were drawn largely from men of high social positions and were able to buy their commissions and promotions.

British soldiers were well-trained professionals, while the Continental Army was made up of men from all professions.

As a rule, the British troops were always better fed than the Americans, with reliable daily rations:

1½ pounds flour or bread
1 pound of beef or a ½ pound of pork
¼ pint of canned peas or 1 ounce of rice
1 ounce of butter
a ration of rum

What About Black Soldiers?

Early in the war, many free blacks volunteered for service with the Continental Army. They were rejected. Slaves weren't allowed either; owners feared that they would expect to be freed based on their military service.

White Americans were mortally afraid of revolt by those they had enslaved. Like most slave owners, Washington dreaded guns in the hands of any blacks. At the start of the war he was opposed to bringing blacks into the army and specifically prohibited it.

★ ★ ★ ★ ★ ★ ★ ★ ★ ★

WASHINGTON CHANGES HIS MIND

Serving by the general's side faithfully throughout the war was William Lee, his manservant and slave, who even accompanied Washington into battle. The war did make the general's views more enlightened. As it dragged on and on, he accepted blacks, free and enslaved, into his troops. His will directed that his slaves be freed after his death, though Martha didn't follow his wishes.

William Lee was George Washington's slave and served him throughout the war.

★ ★ ★ ★ ★ ★ ★ ★ ★ ★

The British attitude toward black soldiers was a stark contrast. In 1775, after the war had begun in Massachusetts, the last British governor of Virginia shocked the patriots with a startling promise. The Royal Governor Lord Dunmore proclaimed that any patriot-owned slave who escaped and fought for the British cause would be emancipated—actively courting slaves by offering them their freedom.

The main motive of the British wasn't a desire to help slaves—though a movement to abolish slavery had succeeded in Britain. But this proclamation was an important part of their military strategy to weaken and destroy the plantations of the American South.

Dunmore sparked one of the great migrations in American history. Tens of thousands of slaves—as many as one hundred thousand—fled from farms, plantations, and cities to try to reach the British camps. About one-third of those who ran away were women. Whole families seized the chance to escape.

About twenty thousand African Americans served with the British troops. Virginia's Ethiopian Regiment—mostly African Americans who had been granted their freedom by Dunmore's proclamation—wore a patch on their uniforms that read, " Liberty to Slaves."

Enslaved Americans chose a side in the Revolution, the side of the Crown. They saw that a British victory, not American independence, offered the best prospects for freedom. Independence would only result in more power for the whites who had enslaved them.

In Virginia, Dunmore's proclamation had the effect of uniting whites behind the patriot effort. Someone traveling through the area wrote, "The inhabitants of this colony are deeply alarmed at this infernal scheme. It seems to quicken all in revolution to overpower [Dunmore] at any risk."

Fury among whites at Dunmore's action was such that Jefferson had included it as a grievance in the Declaration of Independence. He lost thirty of his own slaves during the war, and other Founders lost some of theirs.

RACISM

Most, but not all, of the white colonists accepted racism as the natural order of things, believing that people other than whites were inferior. Many ardently supported the system of enslaving blacks; others were torn but didn't do much to stop it. Most of the powerful white men at the time owned slaves. But some made the choice not to, like John and Abigail Adams, who believed slavery was simply morally wrong.

Meanwhile, again in stark contrast, Georgia and South Carolina were promising a free slave to any new white recruit.

Later in the war, when voluntary enlistments were low, various colonies finally offered freedom to slaves who fought. About seven thousand African Americans served on the Continental side. A few were in all-black regiments, but most were in integrated units. The heroes of some of the key moments in the war included black Americans and former slaves.

What About Indian Nations?

In places like Upstate New York, western Pennsylvania, and the Carolina frontier, warfare was particularly brutal and involved many Indian groups. As with everything, Indian tribes varied in their reactions to the war. Some didn't choose sides and continued to battle one another. Most tribes went with the British or stayed neutral; only a small minority backed the Continental side.

Various economic and political factors were at play, like appreciating the British proclamation banning colonists from moving west onto Indian lands. This led four of the six tribes of the powerful Iroquois Confederacy to side with the British at the outbreak of the war.

Yet several tribes sided with the patriots, including the other two tribes of the Iroquois Confederacy, the Oneidas and the Tuscaroras. This split ended up breaking up the Iroquois Confederacy, with the group gradually losing its power.

What About Women?

Washington and just about everyone else disapproved of women soldiers. Women who attempted to enlist were usually discovered and refused. If they were found out later, they could be punished by prison, whipping, and other torture.

But many women went with their husbands to battle, often taking their children along. Some were afraid to stay at home alone or had no way to support themselves.

Although women were often of great service, working as cooks or laundresses in the camps, foraging for food, and nursing the injured, Washington considered them a nuisance. He lumped them all together as "camp followers," an insulting term. He wouldn't let them ride in wagons with the men—women were supposed to walk alongside. Technically, his own wife, Martha, was a camp follower, but she got to travel by carriage.

★ ★ ★ ★ ★ ★ ★ ★ ★ ★ ★

MARTHA WASHINGTON

Martha Washington became a mother figure to George's troops and kept their spirits up.

A hero in her own right, **Martha Washington** had never been out of Virginia until she started making the arduous journeys to join George wherever he was camped. The sound of guns, riding in a boat, and many other things scared her: "But I endeavor to keep my fears to myself as well as I can."

Martha was the only one who George could be himself around. He depended on her and sought her advice. His troops saw her as a mother figure who sat with them, singing and chatting. She bolstered morale, and admiration for her kept some soldiers from deserting.

Her devotion to the patriot cause was complete. She organized groups of women to make bandages, pack gunpowder, nurse the injured, and do whatever they could do to help. Above all, they knitted socks, which the men desperately needed.

The British hated Martha and once threatened to take her hostage, much to George's fury: "I can hardly think that Lord Dunmore can act so low, and unmanly a part, as to think of seizing Mrs. Washington by way of revenge upon me."

Women received half the food rations that a soldier got, and children got quarter rations. Depending on the jobs women did for the army, they could earn more rations.

Fighting Women

Perhaps three or four women actually served in the army. The most well-known was Deborah Sampson, a Massachusetts woman who disguised herself as Robert Shurtleff and served for over a year. She later became the first woman lecturer in America, regaling audiences with her life story.

Anna Maria Lane was another, Virginia's only female soldier. Anna Maria followed her husband, dressed in men's clothing, and fought in battles with him. After a serious leg wound left her disabled, she raised three children, worked as a nurse in a military hospital, and eventually—and most unusually—received a full military pension.

PAY TO: Jan. 1 1808
Anna Maria Lane
One Hundred Dollars $100.00
Pension

Anna Maria Lane disguised herself as a man and fought
alongside her husband.

★ ★ ★ ★ ★ ★ ★ ★ ★ ★

Many women worked as spies, using their freedom
of movement to gather information and pass it on to the
right people. Two that we know about are Ann Bates of
Philadelphia and Emily Geiger of South Carolina.

Women, of course, were active patriots on the side-
lines, organizing boycotts, raising money for the troops,
nursing, and holding down the fort at home, raising
what were often giant broods of children.

What About Pacifists?

A significant part of the population belonged to religions that didn't believe in war—they preached pacifism. What were they to do?

The largest group was the Quakers, members of the Society of Friends, who had broken away from the established Church of England and, after persecution, had emigrated to the colonies. They were persecuted when they arrived too and were welcome in just a few colonies, notably Pennsylvania. During the war, most Quakers didn't fight—they didn't believe in any violence, including war—but they helped in other ways, caring for the wounded, donating food and blankets. They became the first group in the Western world to ban slaveholding.

Shakers, a new religion in which women had leadership roles, had recently started arriving from England. They openly preached pacifism, calling for colonists to lay down their arms. Naturally they were suspected of being allies of the British. They were feared, hated, and beaten as they spread their views and recruited new members. Their leader, Ann Lee, and others were arrested and jailed. Yet, as some colonists grew disillusioned with the war, they found comfort in this new religion, and the Shakers had established a following by the war's end.

Mennonites were Swiss and German immigrants living mostly in Pennsylvania and places in the Midwest. Committed to pacifism, they didn't choose a side during the war. They were persecuted by patriots, who took away their property as a punishment for not joining militias.

What About Spies?

Spies were actively encouraged and used extensively by both sides throughout the war. Men, women, and even children risked their lives to gather intelligence and pass on information. Secret codes, invisible ink, eavesdropping at coffeehouses and taverns, stealing mail meant for the other side—spies used all the tried-and-true techniques.

Paying for information also worked—Washington was able to get secret funds from Congress to recruit men who would spy for him. Wearing disguises to go behind enemy lines was another patriot favorite—some of the more successful spies pretended to be mentally challenged or emotionally disturbed. Paul Revere and some thirty other men belonged to a group known as the Liberty Boys—an offshoot of the Sons of Liberty—who gathered intelligence on the movement of British troops.

So much spying was taking place that it was actually a challenge for one side to totally surprise the other.

THE MOST FAMOUS SPY

Nathan Hale was a 22-year-old teacher from Connecticut, one of six brothers who served in the war. He was inspired to leave teaching and join the army by his best friend and classmate, Benjamin Tallmadge, who urged: "Was I in your condition, I think the more extensive service would be my choice. Our holy religion, the honor of our God, a glorious country, and a happy constitution is what we have to defend."

When Washington needed a spy to report on British troop movements after they captured New York City, Hale was the only one who volunteered. For the others, going behind enemy lines carried too much risk of being caught and executed. Hale had been serving in the army for a year and ached to do more.

Hale, alas, was still a beginner at spying and lasted only ten days before being recognized at a tavern. He was captured and immediately hanged in September 1776—but not before giving a dignified speech, ending with the famous line: "I only regret that I have but one life to lose for my country."

Nathan Hale risked his life to spy on the British for George Washington.

A Turn for the Worse

In November 1776, after four straight losses in New York and New Jersey, with the British continually forcing him to retreat, Washington was down to three thousand men.

As he wrote to Congress, "The situation of our affairs is critical and truly alarming." Men were going as long as two days with no food and tying rags to their feet in lieu of having shoes. Throughout the war, Congress was consistently unable to raise the funds it needed from the states to support the war effort.

On December 20, Washington wrote, "Ten days more will put an end to the existence of our army."

Still in retreat, his tiny band crossed the Delaware River and set up their gloomy camp in Pennsylvania.

He set his sights on the New Jersey town across the river from camp: Trenton, an isolated fort under control of the British, guarded by 1,200 Germans.

With information gleaned from a spy he had planted, Washington planned his attack.

On a piece of paper, he wrote, "Victory or Death."

CHAPTER 11

Keeping the Flame of the Revolution Alive

It was a wretched Christmas night. December 25, 1776, was bitterly cold with a terrible combination of snow and rain and hail.

But weather didn't halt Washington's new plan of attack.

That sturdy group of Massachusetts fishermen who'd helped him save his troops at the Battle of Long Island (see p. 117) again put their oars to work. In one of the most famous moments of the war, they ferried the troops, their horses, and their weapons across the Delaware River, chunky with ice.

The night was so ugly that it was three in the morning before all made it across. In fact, the danger meant that some were forced to stay behind—Washington was down to 2,400 soldiers. Miraculously, no one died during the crossing.

WASHINGTON CROSSING THE DELAWARE

The crossing was such an iconic symbol that it was painted years later, in 1851, by a German artist, Emanuel Leutze. He got a few things wrong. The flag in the painting was not created until a year later. A different type of boat was used. The men weren't carrying weapons, which were transported separately. The crossing took place in darkness, so there's a little too much light in the picture. And George appears much older than his 44 years. Still, the painting is beloved and now hangs in New York's Metropolitan Museum of Art.

Then the men began the nine-mile march to Trenton. They were walking into the wind and on slippery mud; two men died. In some places the snow turned a dark red from the men whose feet were bleeding. Civilians who knew the terrain joined the march and led the way.

Their commander never wavered. An officer wrote in his diary, "I have never seen Washington so determined as he is now. . . . He is calm and collected."

Washington Triumphs

Luck, in the form of weather, was on his side. Ordinarily, German soldiers would have been out patrolling the roads. But the weather made them wimps, and they were snug indoors. Who would dare approach in such weather?

So the Continental Army's attack at dawn on December 26 took the British by total surprise. Washington was able to surround the town with men and cannons and then take over the fort. With nowhere to go, the enemy tried to escape into local houses, but the patriot women inside started firing at them from their windows.

BRAVE WOMEN

"We may destroy all the men in America, and we shall still have all we can do to defeat the women," said General Charles Cornwallis. He had served under both Gage and Howe and now had a leading role in the British campaign.

The victory that day in the Battle of Trenton was quick. All the leaders in charge were shot, and the whole army surrendered. Washington took nearly one thousand prisoners as well as their provisions: weapons, lots of food and alcohol, much-needed boots.

ALCOHOL

Most Americans then drank large quantities of alcohol, and the army was no exception. Said Washington: "The benefits arising from the moderate use of strong liquor have been experienced in all armies and are not to be disputed." During especially hard times, he doubled the men's alcohol ration when he could.

One week later he won a battle against British reinforcements in the Battle of Princeton, New Jersey. It was another quick victory.

With these victories he wasn't just scoring points. He was boosting troop morale and attracting much-needed recruits.

Washington was doing more than any other single person to keep the flame of the American Revolution alive.

A Tough Winter

The Continental Army proceeded to Morristown, New Jersey, where they stayed from January 6 to May 28, 1777. This was a safe place where they could defend themselves and also be close to New York in case they were needed.

But that winter Morristown was a magnet for snow. Enduring more than twenty snowstorms, the men were reduced to eating roasted shoe leather, tree bark, and dogs.

Washington ordered the men to get the new smallpox vaccine, one of his smartest decisions. Many more men were dying from disease than battle injuries. Martha bravely volunteered to be among the first to get the shot, reassuring soldiers who distrusted vaccines. George himself was immune, having had a bout earlier in his life (with some scars on his face to prove it).

SMALLPOX

This infectious, disfiguring disease was a huge killer in early America. Even while America was trying to grow itself, smallpox would strike and kill off chunks of the population. In 1721, one epidemic of it killed almost one out of ten people in Boston. "Cures" for it were based on superstition, often weird, and always ineffective.

Cotton Mather and one of his slaves, Onesimus,
discuss how a vaccine can cure a disease.

Then came the vaccine, which the Puritan preacher Cotton Mather learned about from one of his African slaves, Onesimus. It involved placing a tiny amount of infected material under the skin, causing a slight case of the disease that would then render the person immune to it. The inoculation was counterintuitive and controversial and had to be pushed by early scientists like Ben Franklin.

"Liberty Mad"

The Trenton-Princeton victories cheered up the Americans and saved the struggle for independence from collapse. Thousands of new soldiers joined up with Washington.

One loyalist was heard to mutter, "Now they are all liberty mad again."

Washington for one was breathing a giant sigh of relief: "This is a glorious day for our country."

But the relief was temporary. There was still no clear path to an eventual victory. Just one bruising skirmish after another, neither side ever decisively ahead.

The majority of the war was fought in New York, New Jersey, and South Carolina, with more than two hundred separate skirmishes and battles occurring in each of these three colonies. But battles were fought in every one of the thirteen colonies, with additional military actions taking place in the future states of Tennessee, Arkansas, Indiana, Illinois, Kentucky, Alabama, and Florida.

The length of the war, now dragging into its third year, surprised many. Both Europeans and Indians had expected it to be brief.

What About France?

It had been clear for a while that the colonists were not going to win the war without help. Now it was Ben Franklin to the rescue. He had set off on a secret mission with his grandsons, ages seven and seventeen, pretending they were riding out of Philly and going on a friendly picnic. Instead, they were speeding to a boat and making the six-week crossing to Paris.

Remember the French and Indian War, when Britain kicked France out of the colonies? This was the seed of the Revolution, when Britain started bossing the colonies around and they didn't like it.

So France was an old enemy of Britain and the best bet for the help the colonies desperately needed. And Franklin was even more beloved in France than he was in the colonies for his work in science, making discoveries about lightning and electricity. Electricians in France were known as *les franklinistes*.

Franklin was famous in France for his work in science.

At first the French, like everyone else, didn't believe there was a chance of America winning. They needed more proof, *s'il vous plaît*.

So Franklin was using his considerable charm on them, all the while surrounded by British spies. Electricity, his specialty, was a brand-new and little-understood topic then. The British, less scientifically curious than the French, were having nightmares. Wild rumors flared that he was cooking up some giant electric weapon to blow up Britain or setting up a system of mirrors that would burn down the British fleet. Mostly, though, Franklin was just going to dinner parties.

BEN FRANKLIN EVERYWHERE AT ONCE

Besides his total of nine years in France, and all his input on founding American documents, Franklin also loaned his own money to help the troops and worked overtime to make sure they got the smallpox vaccine—a scientific cause he was passionate about ever since his beloved son Franky died of the disease at age four.

A Flag!

From its temporarily safe spot in Philadelphia, the Second Continental Congress was trying to manage the war effort as best it could.

On June 14, America finally got its own flag when Congress passed the Flag Resolution: "That the flag of the thirteen United States be thirteen stripes, alternate red and white; that the union be thirteen stars, white in a blue field, representing a new constellation." The red represented strength and bravery, blue symbolized justice and perseverance, and white stood for purity. Anxious to raise morale, flag makers and upholsterers all over Philly got busy sewing to get flags out to troops.

The first flag represented the colonies with thirteen stripes and thirteen stars.

BETSY ROSS

Did a patriotic Philly upholsterer named Betsy Ross really design and make the first flag? Those looking for heroes and heroines of the American Revolution have wanted to think so. Ross learned how to sew from her great-aunt, then worked as an upholsterer's apprentice, and later ran her own business with her husband. For the army she made tents and blankets and repaired uniforms. But it wasn't until 1870, 34 years after her death, that her grandson came forward with the flag claim. For lack of other evidence, today's historians doubt it.

Betsy Ross was at one point called the woman who designed and made the first flag.

Onward to Saratoga

The first Battle of Saratoga, New York (Freeman's Farm), on September 19, 1777, was a draw.

The Continental Army faced British General Burgoyne and fiercely defended their fort, raining fire down at the British troops from tall trees. One of Washington's best and most trusted generals, Benedict Arnold, "acted like a madman" in his aggressive attacks. A thousand men on both sides were shot, and neither side won.

Afterward, the tension was unbearable. The British were expecting reinforcements—which never came—while the Americans anticipated a second attack. As they waited, they listened to the sounds of wolves digging up the bodies buried in shallow graves.

WASHINGTON TRIES TO EASE THE STRESS

As a civilian, George loved plays and went to the theater whenever he had a chance. His favorite play was Joseph Addison's *Cato*, about a noble Roman soldier who kills himself to save his country. Some men set up a small theater in their camp to perform plays, including *Cato*. George and Martha never missed a performance.

George Washington's favorite play was *Cato*.

On October 7 came the second Battle of Saratoga (Bemis Heights), with heavy fighting.

This time the Americans won decisively, led on the battlefield by Arnold yelling, "Rush on, my brave boys!"

The Burgoyne Surrender Dance

By October 17, the British had run out of food. General Burgoyne had no choice but to surrender his entire army of 5,700 British and German soldiers.

To hold the defeated men, America established its first prisoner-of-war camps, in Virginia and Pennsylvania. Conditions there were so dreadful that many died while in captivity.

The British were stunned to see the bedraggled nature of the men who had beat them—shoeless, filthy, and many of them mere boys. The Americans were surprised to see all the animals—raccoons, beavers—the enemy had collected from nearby forests and made into pets.

YANKEE DOODLE AND MORE

"Yankee Doodle" was originally a British song and intended to mock the colonists—"Yankee" was a word of contempt for New Englanders, and "doodle" meant fool. But at that time American troops embraced the tune as their own and bellowed it as the British surrendered at Saratoga.

Then, as now, people wrote popular songs expressing their thoughts about current events. Songs were almost a kind of guerrilla weapon—as soon as one side wrote a ballad, the other side would mock it in a new version. One American song was "The Liberty Song": "Come, join hand in hand, brave Americans all,/And rouse your bold hearts at fair Liberty's call." Within months, British parodies of it began appearing.

The upset was the Americans' first major victory—and the turning point of the war.

John Adams wrote, "The news of Burgoyne's surrender lifted us up to the stars."

On September 26, three weeks earlier, other British troops had taken over Philadelphia, and Congress had fled to York. At night, uneasy in their new homes, Congressmen and their wives did a new dance they called "Burgoyne's Surrender."

The British surrender was the colonies' first major victory.

And in France

Over in France, this victory was finally the deciding factor. These Americans had what it took to found a whole new country. An ecstatic Franklin rushed the news to the palace of King Louis XVI, who promptly said, "Assure the Congress of my friendship. I hope this will be for the good of the two nations."

The French had secretly furnished financial and material aid since 1776. Now they prepared fleets and armies—their support was official and aboveboard.

But victory was still a long way off.

LETTERS FROM WASHINGTON

Besides watching the plays the men put on for him, the general relieved his stress by throwing balls with them, proud of his sturdy right arm muscles. But above all he liked to stay up, while all around him men slept, and scribble letters to a wide assortment of people. He wrote letters begging Congress for funds, letters about getting ready to "bring on a rumpus" with the redcoats. In a famous letter to Phillis Wheatley, the first African-American woman to publish her poetry, he praised her work and invited her to visit him.

Most especially he wrote home, instructing others how to take care of his beloved Mount Vernon. He and Martha were horribly homesick, but never thought of abandoning their responsibilities.

Starting on December 19, Washington and his army of eleven thousand wintered in Valley Forge, twenty-five miles from Philly. It was a dreary winter, the men suffering from lack of food and clothes. One could follow a trail of blood from naked feet over ice. Horses dropped dead from starvation, with men too weak to bury them. Disease ran wild.

A Particularly Anxious Letter from Washington

From December 1777: "I am now convinced beyond a doubt, that, unless some great and capital change suddenly takes place . . . this army must inevitably be reduced to one or other of these three things; starve, dissolve, or disperse."

If the British had decided to attack Valley Forge then, the war would have been over.

But British General William Howe and his troops had taken over the best houses in Philly. They were drinking champagne and living in style, warm and toasty.

The British believed real gentlemen didn't fight war during winter.

CHAPTER 12

And More War

That 1778 winter at Valley Forge was a nightmare. Out of his eleven thousand men, more than 2,500 died from starvation, disease, or the cold. Washington despaired, unable to wrangle money or supplies from the bankrupt Congress.

But something good happened during the miserable winter. Friedrich von Steuben, volunteering on behalf of the French, was a former German army officer with years of experience. He started training the unruly troops. Through constant drills, the men gained confidence and became more of a team.

The war limped along with one battle after another, neither side in a position to declare victory.

Foreign Notables

Besides von Steuben, the Americans had help from other Europeans.

At age nineteen, Marquis de Lafayette offered his military service to our army, making the journey here from France. With his passionate belief in the American Revolutionary cause, he was made a major general and became a valued member of Washington's staff. The Frenchman was appalled at our system of slavery and Washington's reluctance to use black soldiers. But the two developed a father-son-like relationship and were seldom seen apart. Lafayette was skilled and heroic in battle, and helpful in lobbying King Louis XVI for support.

Thaddeus Kosciuszko, a Polish military engineer, was a hero for designing and building forts for the troops. His personal assistant was Agrippa Hull, one of the first free black men to enlist after Washington finally began allowing them in May 1777.

Kosciuszko

Hull

Thaddeus Kosciuszko and Agrippa Hull both helped the war effort.

A Turning Tide?

On June 18, 1778, the British abandoned Philadelphia, going back to the job of attacking the American army. British General William Howe had resigned, replaced by Henry Clinton.

The Continental Army was ready for them, marching confidently out of Valley Forge. Americans attacked Clinton's army in the Battle of Monmouth, New Jersey, on June 28.

But the day went badly. The American general that Washington had put in charge, Charles Lee, disobeyed his orders and retreated instead of keeping up the attack.

Washington raced up to Lee and swore at him, which was just about the only time anyone ever heard him curse.

While the frustrated general tried to reorganize his troops, the temperature soared past 100 degrees. The day ended with no real winner, just many men suffering from heat exhaustion.

MOLLY PITCHERS

There was probably no one woman named Molly Pitcher, say most historians. But the name came to refer to women who carried pitchers of water to heat-stricken men on the battlefield. They became symbols of women's bravery in the war. At least one of them took over her husband's cannon after he was shot. Artists have painted her often; the sketchy details about her mean she always looks different.

But the tide was turning, thanks to Ben Franklin and foreign aid.

So far, the conflict had been technically a civil war within the British Empire. Now it was becoming an international war as:

- France joined in 1778
- Spain in 1779
- and the Netherlands in 1780

Besides contributing money and resources, all three countries used their naval power, far superior to the colonies', to battle the British at sea. This put Britain in a position of fighting a war in way too many places at once, with no allies. It should have signaled the beginning of the end for them.

Still, by the end of 1778, the American Revolution was far from over. In the North, the war had stalemated. All the British had to show so far was control of New York City.

Then, in 1779, battles took place in South Carolina and Georgia; plus Vincennes, Indiana; and many other places.

The battle was long and spread across all the colonies.

Foxes in the Swamps

The British were focusing more and more on the South, capturing large parts of Georgia and South Carolina, in the not-always-correct belief that more loyalist supporters were there to help. The king had persisted in thinking the Southern states were his friends. But his troops were doing so much looting that many loyalists were turning into patriots.

Plus, the South was largely swampland, and this is where guerrilla warfare won the day.

In South Carolina, a man known as the Swamp Fox

was making himself legendary and the British soldiers miserable. With his irregular tactics, the Swamp Fox was so ruthless and basically unbeatable that the British were never able to gain complete control of the area.

The Mysterious Swamp Fox

His real name was Francis Marion, and at 25 he had joined the South Carolina militia to fight in the French and Indian War. While battling—and almost losing to—the Cherokee Indians, he admired how the Cherokee turned the swampy backwoods to their advantage, hiding until just the right moment for an ambush. Twenty years later, he used Cherokee techniques to help the American cause. With small groups of men (both black and white) he would attack without warning, then quickly disappear into the swamps. The British loathed him. His men, known as Marion's Men, loved him. They served without pay and brought their own weapons and horses. Their successful skirmishes helped keep the spark of the American Revolution alive in the South.

Action at Sea

Naval power wasn't a strong suit for the colonies.

The British navy had been able to capture Savannah, the strategic port city in Georgia, in 1778. Americans tried for months to take it back, with help from France's navy, but the British would control it until almost the end of the war.

Besides having the best army, Britain had the best navy in the world. In 1776, Americans had twenty-seven ships against Britain's 270. By the end of the war, the British total had risen close to five hundred, and the American total had dwindled to twenty.

The official navy may not have been effective, but unofficially privateers (or pirates, depending on your point of view) were. Those commanding their own ships had success in attacking British ships. They were able to put a serious dent in British commerce, capturing vast amounts of property and thousands of British sailors.

The most successful and famous privateer was John Paul Jones. In 1779, his ship captured the HMS *Serapis* off the English coast. Following a bloody battle, the British demanded his surrender—whereupon Jones yelled the immortal line "I have not yet begun to fight!"

One of his sailors tossed a grenade that landed in gunpowder on the *Serapis*, exploding the ship, and it was the British who had to surrender.

More Losses

That winter, Washington's main army went back to Morristown to camp.

In 1780, the British took control of Charleston, South Carolina, then the fourth-largest city in the colonies. General Clinton cut off the city from relief and, after a brief attack, forced it to surrender on May 12.

This was the most stunning British victory of the war. The loss of Charleston and its five thousand troops—virtually the entire Continental Army in the South—was a serious blow to the American cause.

Then, on August 16, came the Battle of Camden, South Carolina. The Americans lost—badly. The crushing defeat of the Continental Army there stands out as the deadliest battle of the war. Approximately 1,050 Continental troops were killed and wounded, while the British suffered only 314 casualties.

Betrayal

As if this all wasn't enough, the Americans found trouble coming from even within their own troops.

In the summer of 1780, one of Washington's very favorite men, General Benedict Arnold, betrayed him. Having hatched a plan to get the British to pay him for switching sides, he took command of the fort at West Point, then conspired with British officer John André, assistant to General Clinton.

Arnold wrote down the plans for how the British could take over West Point, which Washington considered the most strategic spot of the whole war. André hid the papers in his boot. But on his way to deliver the papers, André was captured by Americans. They searched him and promptly got those papers to Washington.

So the attack was foiled, and André was arrested for spying and hanged.

But Washington was so stunned at the disloyalty of one of his generals that he was shaking.

THE TEACHER WHO AIDED WASHINGTON

Washington had several talented men assisting him, and one was Major Benjamin Tallmadge, a former teacher. Tallmadge was galvanized into patriot action by the execution of his best friend, Nathan Hale. He had a key role as the head of Washington's network of spies in and around

New York City. It was Tallmadge who played a crucial part in the capture of John André, which revealed Benedict Arnold's treasonous plan to turn over the fort at West Point to the British.

Benjamin Tallmadge was the head of Washington's network of spies.

★ ★ ★ ★ ★ ★ ★ ★ ★ ★

Arnold narrowly escaped to New York to the British side. He was commissioned into their army as a general, but he wasn't all that welcome. He had betrayed his own country for money—making the British suspicious of him.

Said one leader, "Officers have conceived such an aversion to him that they unanimously refused to serve under his command."

★ ★ ★ ★ ★ ★ ★ ★ ★ ★

BENEDICT ARNOLD

Arnold would have been considered a major hero of the war, except for one thing. He had taken part in the Ethan Allen raid and had become Washington's favorite general. Washington thought of Arnold as active, spirited, and sensible. Others saw him as arrogant, death-defying, and a bit full of himself. In the Battles of Saratoga, he charged so aggressively that some thought he was possessed by demons. While fighting, Arnold suffered a serious injury when his horse was shot from under him and then fell on him. His leg was fractured.

During his recovery, his pride and arrogance seemed to fester. He was frustrated at the lack of recognition from Congress for his bravery and resentful that he was being passed over for promotions. He was also short of money, and seemed to have nudged himself into a place where betraying his country sounded like a good thing. He enters history books as the most famous of those who switched sides during this chaotic war.

Benedict Arnold could have been known as a war hero,
but instead he is known as a traitor.

★ ★ ★ ★ ★ ★ ★ ★ ★ ★

Had Benedict Arnold succeeded—and he very nearly did—Washington would have been sent to Britain and hanged.

Once again, the war would have been lost.

Instead, Congress created a day of national thanksgiving that the plan had failed. And the close call united Washington's loyal troops behind him more than ever.

Now if only he could mount a major, decisive attack.

CHAPTER 13

The World Turned Upside Down

It was now 1781. Six years into the war that . . . wouldn't . . . end.

In the South, Nathanael Greene, possibly Washington's most trusted general, was commanding what remained of the Southern Continental Army. His strategy was simple: to wear down General Cornwallis's men by chasing them all over North and South Carolina, engaging in small battles along the way.

By the summer of 1781, Cornwallis had had enough. Half of his troops were incapacitated by malaria, a disease most Americans were immune to.

He took his 8,000 soldiers up to Virginia, continuing to skirmish. He gained control of Yorktown, a port town on the Chesapeake Bay where he could move his men in and out of New York as needed.

But little did he know he was now trapped there.

JAMES ARMISTEAD

James Armistead was an African American slave serving as a spy in the Continental Army under Marquis de Lafayette.

At first, Armistead joined the camp of Benedict Arnold, bringing back useful information about the traitor's movements. Then he volunteered to enter the camp of Cornwallis and act as the commander's personal waiter. While relaxing at the table, the British talked openly in front of him—the perfect spot to gather the juiciest information about strategy.

He had the brilliant idea of becoming a double agent—pretending to spy on the Americans and feeding Cornwallis the wrong information. He made written reports that helped them find out all about what was going on at Yorktown—enabling victory.

James Armistead became a double agent and helped the
Americans win key victories.

Everyone was sick of the war by this time.

Even Washington was starting to crack, having to
apologize for rudeness to his brilliant young assistant,
Alexander Hamilton.

ALEXANDER HAMILTON

Hamilton began life as a poor orphan from the West Indies, but young
as he was, he was already making a name for himself on the strength
of his writing. He had earned Washington's absolute trust and become
his right-hand man. Over the course of four years, he helped the commander in chief in a wide range of duties, especially in conveying
instructions to the generals.

After the war, Hamilton remained in public service as a popular politician, going on to help design the new American government and economy. Most admired him, but he did have enemies. At 47, he was shot and killed in a duel with vice president Aaron Burr, who thus made himself a candidate for most hated man in American history.

Alexander Hamilton became Washington's right-hand man and later helped to design the new government and economy.

Alexander Hamilton has become trendier than ever with Lin-Manuel Miranda's hit Broadway musical *Hamilton*—which is actually an enjoyable way of understanding this era.

Washington's Next Move

Washington was camped just north of New York City, his troops beefed up with four hundred French soldiers. He spent all his time studying maps, looking for a weak spot to attack.

Suddenly, he saw one. He decided to take his army

450 miles south, to the very place where Cornwallis's troops were settling in: Yorktown, Virginia.

Cleverly, he left behind enough evidence—like functioning bakeries to make it look like troops were being fed and sending out fake messages about where he was going—to lead the British to think his troops were still in New York, planning an attack on the city.

And Cornwallis was unaware that Lafayette and his troops were shadowing him the whole time. Lafayette was helping to pin Cornwallis in place.

Also helping was the fleet of twenty-eight French warships headed to Yorktown, blocking a British escape by sea.

Washington had no way to communicate with the ships. On the day that the French admiral arrived in a rowboat, Washington was so gleeful that, in an exceptionally rare move, he hugged the Frenchman.

Showdown at Yorktown

The Siege of Yorktown began on September 28, with Washington surrounding the British by land, the French by sea. No one was coming to Cornwallis's rescue.

"We have got him handsomely in a pudding bag," one of Washington's generals gloated. Washington fired the first shot himself. He gave the order to keep the gunfire going all night and then to begin blasting cannonballs.

The British troops fired back as best they could. For them, this was the most shocking moment of the whole war.

Washington watched the bombardment closely. When an officer told him to step back for his own safety, he refused. After six long years, he did not want to miss a minute of that day's action.

The World Turned Upside Down

Weeks passed, with the French and Americans competing to see who could inflict the most damage to the British army. Just eighty-eight men were killed on the American side. The British grew weaker and weaker. Their situation was hopeless.

Washington began seeing dead horses in the water. This told him that the British didn't even have enough food to feed their animals.

Finally, a teen drummer emerged, followed by a British officer waving a white handkerchief. The British were going to surrender!

The British officially surrendered in October 1781.

On October 19, 1781, General Cornwallis officially surrendered, not deigning to appear in person. As his eight thousand men came forward, they made a point of smashing down their guns hard enough to try to damage them.

A witness said, "Some bit their lips; some pouted; others cried."

All were taken as prisoners of war. For the second time during the war (following Burgoyne's surrender in 1777), the British had lost an entire army. And this time, the war.

As an American flag waved high, the British marching band played a weirdly appropriate song called "The World Turned Upside Down"—which indeed for them it had.

Washington dashed off a note to Congress while celebrations began all throughout America.

The shock echoed to London.

Only King George III remained in denial. He actually wanted to persist with the war, and when he was talked out of it by his advisers, he tried to resign.

He simply had to accept it: his time as ruler over the colonies had come to an end.

CHAPTER 14

Surprising the Whole World

But wait—this wasn't the end of the British-American conflict.

Now the peace talks between the two countries began. John Adams, Ben Franklin, and others left for the French capital of Paris to represent America.

Believe it or not, failure was still possible. Both sides had to agree to the terms. Hammering out all the details was going to take two more years.

And in the meantime, military action in the colonies continued. In 1782, the British troops began evacuating the South, still skirmishing as they left.

HEARTS OF PURPLE

In 1782, Washington established the Badge of Military Merit, the first military award of the new country, the first time an award had been given to ordinary soldiers. As he said, the "road to glory in a patriot army and a free country is thus open to all." He awarded it to three of his best men.

Now known as the Purple Heart, for soldiers wounded or killed in the line of duty, it has been given to over a million military members since.

The purple heart is one of the most recognized and respected medals awarded to members of the US military.

After France, the Dutch Republic (Netherlands), and Spain were the first to recognize America as a new country. Morocco and other countries began following their lead.

And Then Mutiny

Poor Washington never got a break. As his troops continued to battle in the North, morale was sinking: "You may rely upon it," he wrote, "the patience and long sufferance of this army are almost exhausted, and that there never was so great a spirit of discontent as at this instant."

Finally, his troops in Newburgh, New York, began to conspire against him. They were understandably weary of fighting, exhausted, bored—and very worried. There was still a chance the peace talks could fail, and if they did, how were the soldiers going to get the money they were owed?

Congress was still bankrupt. Many men hadn't been paid for so long—in many cases years—that they faced going directly into debtor's prison when they got home.

IN PRISON FOR DEBT

In a counterproductive law carried over from England, those who went into debt were subject to cruel and unusual punishment. They could have their land and property seized and be thrown into jail while their families scrambled to pay the debt. When they were eventually released, they had to "work off" what they still owed. Not until 1833 were debtors prisons banned in America.

The Newburgh Conspiracy was an all-out mutiny, a conspiracy from within, with men threatening to lay down their arms and let Britain take over once more unless they received their pay.

It was Washington once again to the rescue. He professed total sympathy with them, writing of his "men oftentimes half starved; always in rags, without pay, and experiencing, at times, every species of distress which human nature is capable of undergoing."

But a military revolt against the fragile new American government could have been disastrous. It had to be stopped.

To the mutineers, Washington gave one of his best speeches ever in March 1783. He pleaded with them to reject the calls for violence.

Then he concluded by putting on a set of glasses none of them had ever seen before: "Gentlemen, you will permit me to put on my spectacles, for, I have not only grown gray, but almost blind in the service of my country."

George Washington's spectacles

The men not only calmed down and regained their respect in him as a leader who had sacrificed so much for his country—but some of them cried.

The next month, it became clear the treaty talks *were* going to work, with all sides coming closer and closer to agreeing on terms.

Washington ordered an extra ration of alcohol issued to every man in the army, celebrating those who had "assisted in protecting the rights of human nature and establishing an asylum for the poor and oppressed of all nations and religions."

We Grow Up

Finally, on September 3, 1783, the United States and Great Britain signed the Treaty of Paris.

The war was over. The United States was an independent nation. The British Crown could never again interfere.

The treaty was very favorable to the new nation, greatly enlarging its territory with generous boundaries—all the land north of Florida, south of Canada, and east of the Mississippi River.

The Treaty of Paris allowed the new nation to expand its territory.

All prisoners of war were to be released, and any property (including slaves) left behind by the British was to be forfeited.

The new United States were growing up.

FOR THE FICTIONAL SIDE OF THE STORY

Ask your favorite librarian for novels that take place during the Revolutionary War. To name a few: *Johnny Tremain* by Esther Forbes, *My Brother Sam Is Dead* by James Lincoln Collier and Christopher Collier, *Guns for General Washington* by Seymour Reit, and the Seeds of America trilogy by Laurie Halse Anderson.

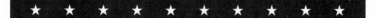

An estimated 15 to 20 percent of the population had remained faithful to the Crown, and they were now on the wrong side of history—losers of the war. For their safety, Great Britain had to get the loyalists out of the country. Thousands of them began evacuating from Savannah, Charleston, and finally New York City.

Washington then reentered the city in triumph.

Farewell

On December 4, Washington said good-bye to his officers at New York's Fraunces Tavern.

Benjamin Tallmadge, faithful aide to Washington, provided the only account of that moment: "Such a scene of sorrow and weeping I had never before witnessed," he said.

Even Washington let his emotions show, allowing the men to hug him. His hand was shaking as he raised his glass of wine, tears rolling down his cheeks. He thanked his troops for coming from diverse areas with "the most violent local prejudices" and reshaping themselves into "one patriotic band of brothers," united in their efforts.

"With a heart full of love and gratitude," he said, "I now take leave of you. I most devoutly wish that your latter days may be as prosperous and happy as your former ones have been glorious and honorable."

Next he resigned as commander, fully intent on retiring to his comfortable home in Mount Vernon, devoting his days to its upkeep.

And yet at this point he was the most popular and admired man in the country—and still theoretically in command of an army. Had he wanted to, he could have seized power for himself—become the new King George of America.

But that was not his way at all—he respected his new country too much.

Instead, marking a classic case of "no rest for the weary," his enjoyable respite at Mount Vernon was all too brief.

Washington *never* said no when he was called to duty. Four years later, in 1787, he reluctantly attended the Constitutional Convention in Philadelphia. He served as a delegate from Virginia, taking on a role in crafting our Constitution, the blueprint for how our new government was to work. So immense was Washington's prestige that the other delegates designed the presidency with him in mind.

So in 1789 he was elected as our first president. He was the unanimous choice of the newly formed Electoral College, made up of representatives from each state—he had no rivals. The job wasn't defined—it was going to be up to him to define it—and he was full of doubts and "anxious and painful sensations."

But once again Washington said yes.

Surprise!

The way the Revolutionary War turned out surprised the whole world. For the first time in history, colonies had broken free of their colonizer.

Victory for America was definitely not inevitable. "The outcome seemed little short of a miracle," wrote one historian.

Some of the reasons why we won:
- luck
- Washington
- the will of the people—the strong belief in our cause
- the French
- mistakes by the British

George Washington, with his immense stamina, just wouldn't give up or go away. Stalwart in adversity, he mastered the art of leadership. He took daring risks and was often able to turn British mistakes to his advantage. Passionately patriotic, he inspired the same spirit in his men and shaped them, more or less, into a unit.

The arrogant British, meanwhile, never developed an overall general strategy for winning the war. They sent comparatively small numbers of troops to America, and although their use of sea power gave them greater flexibility than the Americans, it wasn't enough to compensate for the lack of manpower.

They could have won very early on but didn't use

their power in savvy ways. Too often they chose to minimize their risks, missing opportunities to quash the rebellion. At crucial moments they misunderstood what was going on or failed to cooperate with one another.

Also, the British blundered by counting too much on loyalist support they did not in fact always have.

The British had controlled many key cities within the colonies. But 90 percent of the colonial population lived in rural areas. So the British were able to maintain power only in areas with a strong military presence—cities—and were never able to control the countryside.

For them, fighting the Americans was like punching a pillow—no sooner did a section go down than another popped up.

The supplies and funds furnished by France were a great help, while French military and naval support after 1778 was crucial. The French helped bring about the final British surrender at Yorktown.

One more reason to consider: we had the Declaration of Independence, a masterpiece of rhetoric that gave courage to the new country.

★ ★ ★ ★ ★ ★ ★ ★ ★ ★ ★ ★ ★ ★

WISE WORDS

"I think the notion of our Founders being these perfect men who got these stone tablets from the sky that became our Constitution and Bill of Rights is [wrong]. They did a remarkable thing in sticking the landing from revolution to government. That's the hardest thing to do."

—playwright Lin-Manuel Miranda

★ ★ ★ ★ ★ ★ ★ ★ ★ ★ ★ ★ ★ ★

So the astonishing outcome resulted from a combination of British blunders, French assistance, and American idealism and efforts.

What If America Had Lost?

Again and again, Washington came close to losing his army. There were so many close calls and entirely possible ways in which the colonists could have lost the war. A considerable amount of luck came to the American army—in the form of weather, mistakes on the other side, those red coats, guerrilla tactics that worked surprisingly well, and more.

It's probably unlikely that, once it had sparked, the flame of freedom felt by the patriots could have ever been completely put out.

But had the colonists lost this war, it could have been disastrous. Most historians believe that independence would have taken much longer to achieve, and the struggle would have been much bloodier on both sides. There could have been decades of warfare.

The rebellion might have eventually been crushed, with Britain installing a brutally harsh regime to finish the job. Punishments could have been extreme. All the leaders would have been executed. Colonies would have been forced to pay the costs of the war through unimaginable taxes and the seizure of property. Poverty and widespread famine would have taken over.

In fact, there might never have been a United States.

Those a British Victory Would Have Helped

Slavery in the United States would have been abolished sooner. In England itself, the slave trade was abolished in 1807, and as of 1833, in all its colonies as well. That's decades earlier than in the United States—and unlike in Britain it took a nightmarish Civil War to do it.

The Indians would probably have fared better, too, with the British having more favorable policies toward them.

And without victory, Americans wouldn't have the Declaration of Independence.

The Declaration didn't just announce the separation of thirteen colonies from Great Britain—it was to become the most famous defense of human rights in the world.

CHAPTER 15

What Happened Next?

Though the Americans won, it was at a dreadful cost, with about twenty-five thousand killed, or roughly one percent of the colonial population. In today's terms, that would be the equivalent of a war claiming more than three million American lives.

But the work of building a new nation had begun, with the promise of greater opportunity for all luring streams of new immigrants.

The country would grow and grow. In 1791, Vermont would become the fourteenth state. This was the Green Mountains, that area of America so independent it hadn't even been part of a colony.

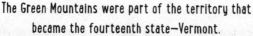

The Green Mountains were part of the territory that became the fourteenth state—Vermont.

PRESERVATION

In 1864, after photography had been invented, six known surviving veterans of the war got their picture taken—all of them over a hundred years old.

While some of the larger battle sites and campsites are preserved as either national or state parks, a surprising number are not or are only partially preserved. Work is ongoing to continue preserving these sites as well as compiling lists of the soldiers who fought in each location.

When photography was invented, veterans of the war began preserving their efforts and historic sites.

Ironically and unsurprisingly, taxes in America soared. They had to be increased in order to fund the war, and then a new national government and military force. They amounted to more taxes than Britain would have dreamed of—and it was still taxation without representation. Only wealthy white property owners could vote at first, not shopkeepers, merchants, craftsmen, farmers, or anyone who couldn't meet the financial requirements: owning property in excess of a certain value.

TAXATION *WITH* REPRESENTATION

Most white men were able to vote by 1828. Black men were granted the right to vote in 1867, but restrictions were often put in their way, until the Voting Rights Act of 1965.

Women weren't allowed to vote until 1920.

The new country had lost the protection of the British king. True, that's what the colonists had once wanted, but there would be times when it would have come in handy.

For example, in the Mediterranean, the pirates of North African countries of the Barbary Coast inflicted constant damage to American ships doing business. The British navy had protected them but no more. The Americans sped up the formation of their own strong navy, but piracy remained a serious problem until 1815.

More Aftereffects

Approximately 7,500 German soldiers had been killed or died of disease. Thousands of those who survived, pleased with their new surroundings, decided to settle in America after the war.

The British lost approximately twenty-four thousand men—killed in battle, from disease, or in the prisoner-of-war camps.

NO NEED TO PITY THE BRITISH EMPIRE

The Empire would have to survive without its intended cornerstone of America—and it did. After its humiliating defeat, it promptly turned its attention elsewhere, collecting other colonies, becoming the largest empire in world history. No longer able to deport its convicts to the American colonies, it began shipping criminals to its new colony of Australia.

By 1922, at its peak, the British Empire ruled over one-fourth of the world's people and one-fourth of its total land area. It truly was an empire on which the "sun never set"—it was always shining on one of its colonies somewhere. Many are proud of the Empire and what it accomplished. Others point to its brutality, the needless deaths and suffering it caused, most notably after it colonized India, the new "jewel in its crown," in 1858. The Empire lost prestige after World War II, and with India achieving independence in 1947, it began to decline.

The loyalist civilians left behind in America had to move somewhere else. This represented a drain of as many as eighty thousand of the more educated and skilled colonists. They lost everything and went back to Britain, fled to the West, or moved to Canada.

The evacuees included thousands of African Americans who had helped the British. Some relocated to freedom in Nova Scotia. Those who didn't like it there left for Africa, where the English had founded a colony for free blacks in Sierra Leone.

The institution of slavery continued to be practiced in the original thirteen colonies. Within days of the war's end, plantation owners were paying soldiers to locate runaway slaves living in the surrounding woods.

But many were starting to question their racism, and ideas about slavery were shifting. In many ways as a result of black heroism and loyalty to the American cause, many northern states outlawed slavery after the war. Vermont was the first new state whose constitution simply prohibited it. In some northern states, free African Americans were granted the right to vote.

Free African Americans were granted the right to vote in some northern states.

But it would take the Civil War and the twentieth-century civil rights movement to make African American equality a priority.

WISE WORDS

"This nation was founded on the idea that some lives don't matter. Freedom and justice for some, not all. That's the foundation. Yes, progress has been made in some respects, but it hasn't come easy. There's an unfinished revolution waiting to be won."

—Michelle Alexander, civil rights lawyer and author

"That's the story of America. An experiment that's not yet finished. A project that belongs to all of us."

—President Barack Obama, 2016

Abigail Adams's "Remember the ladies" did put the topic of the unequal status of women on the table, but it would be years before it was taken seriously. At the crucial gathering of women's rights activists at Seneca Falls in New York in 1848, their declaration had some familiar words: "We hold these truths to be self-evident, that all men and women are created equal."

VICTORIA WOODHULL, FIRST WOMAN TO RUN FOR PRESIDENT

Victoria Woodhull was the first woman to address a
congressional committee, arguing for women's right to vote.

In 1871, Woodhull, a stockbroker and women's rights activist, became
the first woman to address a congressional committee, arguing for wom-
en's right to vote. Women were already tax-paying citizens, she said, and
"the citizen who is taxed should also have a voice in the subject matter
of taxation." No more taxation without representation for women.

Gay Americans have also used the Declaration's language to fight for marriage equality laws, as have black
Americans for their civil rights.

Indian Nations

Indians, though, were unable to prevail. The fate of many Indian nations after the American Revolution was a tragic one. They were completely left out of the Treaty of Paris in 1783. "You are a subdued people," said a treaty commissioner to Iroquois chiefs in 1784—and by 1795 this process of subduing was in full, violent motion. One of the deadliest times was the Trail of Tears, the forced relocation of Cherokee Indians from the Southeast in 1838, during which thousands perished.

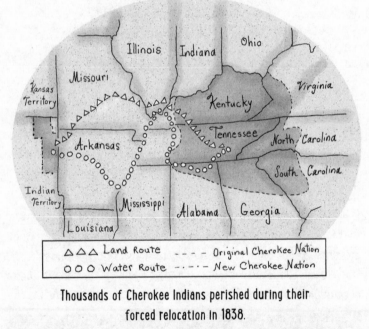

Thousands of Cherokee Indians perished during their forced relocation in 1838.

★ ★ ★ ★ ★ ★ ★ ★ ★ ★

THE INDIAN POPULATION

Fifteen million Indians were here when Christopher Columbus arrived in 1492. By 1900, disease and government cruelty—massacres and being forcibly driven from their land—had reduced that number to 250,000.

But today the population is growing again, with three million people in 500 recognized nations.

Members of the Iroquois Confederacy, along with many other Indian nations, were torn apart by the conflict, weakened by infighting and disease. Treaties made with the British prior to the war were ignored by the Americans, and years of bloody conflict and expansion destroyed some tribes. Tribes like the Ojibwe who had fought for the British had their land taken away.

On the British Side

Benedict Arnold left for London. He remained unpopular, viewed as a money-grubbing traitor, plus a scapegoat for Britain's surprising defeat. So many avenues were closed to him that he tried to start over in Canada, failed, and had to return to London, where he died still a failure: "Poor General Arnold has departed this world without notice," one newspaper did report.

Lord North was forced out of office as prime minister of Great Britain. A Parliamentary motion of no confidence stated that he was no longer fit to hold that position. Today he is mostly remembered as the prime minister who lost America.

King George III's reputation suffered an embarrassing decline. He developed strange symptoms of mental illness never definitively diagnosed, possibly bipolar disease or a blood ailment called porphyria. In his last years, nicknamed "Mad King George," he would not stop talking. His agitation was so severe that doctors kept him in a straightjacket in isolation.

After he died in 1820 at the age of eighty-one, the British monarchy lost much of its actual power and became more symbolic.

What Happened to the Heroes?

Samuel Adams, after his work on the Second Congress, began to fade from history. A key influence in the early days of the Revolution, he's now one of our lesser known Founders. But his cousin John insisted that "without the character of Samuel Adams, the true history of the American Revolution can never be written." Jefferson agreed: "Samuel Adams was the man."

SAMUEL ADAMS AND BEER

Samuel's father had once owned the largest brewery in Boston, and today his name is mainly remembered as a brand of beer. The Boston Beer Company started manufacturing Samuel Adams beer in 1984—a bit rude because Adams didn't particularly like to drink. And the portrait on the beer's label isn't even of him but Paul Revere.

With nine terms as governor, **John Hancock** remained the most popular man in Massachusetts for the rest of his life.

George Washington, as our first president, continued to act heroically during his two terms in office, making a difficult act for future presidents to follow.

George and Martha finally got to go back home to Mount Vernon for good in 1797, where he died two years later.

Martha Washington established precedent as our first First Lady. She didn't like to complain, but she wasn't fond of the job: "I think I am more like a state prisoner than anything else, there is certain bounds set for me which I must not depart from." The routine of the president's spouse was a bit dull after all the action of war. But Martha never shirked her duty, putting on an act of enjoying herself that convinced all around her. She continued to have a strong bond with the soldiers, helping war veterans as much as she could. Any vet who came to pay his respects to George or ask for favors and was unable to see him was thrilled to see her instead.

John Adams, still quarrelsome and tactless, had done so much for the country that he went on to be vice president under Washington and then our second president. He died at ninety, on a July Fourth.

Abigail Adams, as our second First Lady, continued to be considered her husband's most trusted adviser. She attended debates on the floor of Congress and discussed everything with him. She was much bolder than Martha about giving her opinions. She remained keenly interested in politics for the rest of her life. She died at seventy-three, not living to see her son John Quincy Adams become the sixth president.

Thomas Jefferson went on to become the first secretary of state, the second vice president, and our third president. Retiring to Monticello, he was busier than ever with all of his projects, including keeping detailed notes on his wine purchases. He died in debt, also on a July Fourth.

★ ★ ★ ★ ★ ★ ★ ★ ★ ★ ★

FUTURE PRESIDENTS

James Monroe played a role in the revolution and later became our fifth president.

Many figures famous in later American history played a role in the Revolution when they were young. **James Monroe** crossed the Delaware with Washington, was wounded at Trenton, and later became our fifth president. He named a policy for himself—the Monroe Doctrine—which held that any attempt by European countries to establish colonies in the United States would be considered an act of war. His wife, Elizabeth, played a crucial role in saving the wife of Marquis de Lafayette from certain execution during the French Revolution.

Andrew Jackson, a young boy during the Revolution, acted as a messenger and was captured by the British. As a prisoner of war, Jackson nearly starved, contracted smallpox, and was slashed by a British officer after refusing to clean his boots. He later defeated John Quincy Adams (John and Abigail's son) in the race to become our seventh president. As such, he did more than any other president to forcibly remove Indians from their land.

Benjamin Franklin returned from France as a hero and settled back in Philadelphia, where he spent his remaining years helping the nation, founding a society for the abolition of slavery, and doing some science on the side.

Ethan Allen was captured as a British prisoner of war, but was eventually freed to return to his beloved Vermont.

Patrick Henry continued to serve the new nation on the battlefield, in politics, and in courtrooms until he died. In serious debt, he had seventeen children.

Thomas Paine continued to agitate here, in Britain, and in France. He too died in major debt.

Mercy Otis Warren went on to write a three-volume history of the Revolution, the first history of the war written by a woman. Said Alexander Hamilton: "In the career of dramatic composition at least, female genius in the United States has outstripped the male."

Paul Revere went back to life as a silversmith and owner of a hardware store but never stopped fighting for his country. In the War of 1812, at age seventy-seven, he helped to fortify Boston. Sometimes called a "do-over," this was *another* war for independence from Great Britain (we won this one, too).

James Armistead won his freedom after the war and chose to add "Lafayette" as his last name. The bond between the two men remained close: when Lafayette came back for a visit in 1824, he saw Armistead in the crowd and leaped out of his carriage to hug him.

Marquis de Lafayette returned to France as a hero, helped lead the French Revolution, and eventually visited America, where he was greeted with great fanfare. While in New Orleans, he met with African-American veterans and continued to speak out about the contradiction between America's ideals about freedom and its system of keeping others in captivity.

DAUGHTERS AND SONS OF THE AMERICAN REVOLUTION

Sons of the American Revolution (www.sar.org) was the first organization of descendants of the patriots, established in 1889. Members have to prove bloodline descent from an ancestor who actively supported the war. The organization sponsors historical research and raises funds for the preservation of sites and documents.

But the Sons refused to allow women to join, so in 1890, women founded Daughters of the American Revolution (www.dar.org), now a more famous organization. It promotes preservation, education, patriotism, and honoring our patriots. The organization was initially for white women, and became notorious in 1939 for refusing to allow the famed African American singer Marian Anderson to perform at DAR Constitution Hall. They changed their "white performers only" policy in 1952 and began admitting African American members in 1977. Now they focus on racial diversity, with publications like *Forgotten Patriots—African American and American Indian Patriots in the Revolutionary War.*

CHAPTER 16

The Power of the Declaration

They might be the most significant five words ever written in America: "All men are created equal."

The Declaration of Independence is our glittering touchstone, the document that marks the beginning of our history as a people. Setting out the principles that drove the subjects of King George III to revolt against him, it was the first formal assertion by a whole people of their right to a government of their own choice.

★ ★ ★ ★ ★ ★ ★ ★ ★ ★ ★ ★ ★ ★

WISE WORDS

"Our founding documents were genius. But not because they were perfect. They were saddled with the imperfections and even the bigotry of the past. Native Americans were referred to as savages, black Americans were referred to as fractions of human beings, and women were not mentioned at all.

But those facts and other ugly parts of our history don't detract from our nation's greatness. In fact, I believe we are an even greater nation, not because we started perfect, but because every generation has successfully labored to make us a more perfect union. Generations of heroic Americans have made America more inclusive, more expansive, and more just."

—Senator Cory Booker, 2016

★ ★ ★ ★ ★ ★ ★ ★ ★ ★ ★ ★ ★ ★

The Declaration has also served as a sacred, resilient text for later generations of Americans.

It is well worth studying for what it had to say in its own time and what it might have to say to us today.

The Mysterious Handprint

The original Declaration is on display at the National Archives in Washington, DC. Over the years it was not always treated with the utmost care—no one has ever explained the dirty handprint on the bottom left corner. It's now sealed in a titanium-and-aluminum frame with controlled humidity and special lighting.

Phrases of the Declaration have shaped the United States, in particular "life, liberty, and the pursuit of happiness." Endlessly debated, the Declaration has worked to justify the extension of American political and social democracy.

In this country we have a promise to uphold that each generation will have a better life than the previous one, and that's what the Declaration allows us to work toward. It became a springboard for those left out to move ahead and work toward equality.

Wise Words

"The Declaration of Independence stands at the core of our country's origins, a remarkable and enduring achievement. . . . It was the first document of its kind to propose a governing authority deriving from the consent of the governed. . . .

If we are to survive as a nation, it is critical that our citizenry know and understand the beliefs and tenets that underwrite the Declaration of Independence. Its self-evident truths continue to resonate with millions of Americans, as well as with people all around the globe."

—Supreme Court Justice Sandra Day O'Connor

It has kept America stable as the country has gone on to draw millions of new people. Because of this crucial document, the United States became a haven for immigrants, continuing with European countries, expanding to countries from around the world, hopeful people seeking a better life according to the Declaration's promises. No more kings and aristocracy but talent and a willingness to work hard were going to shape the economy for the benefit of a greater number of people.

WISE WORDS

"Since the beginning of the great unfinished symphony that is our American experiment, time and time again, immigrants get the job done."
—playwright Lin-Manuel Miranda

An ongoing controversy concerns recent new immigrants, mostly from Mexico and Central American countries, who enter the country illegally. Some politicians want to close the borders and deport them—currently around eleven million people. Others want to establish a path for them to become citizens—a solution seemingly more in line with the Declaration.

Also in the news is the wave of Muslim immigrants from the Middle East, in particular refugees from war-torn Syria. The screening process they must go through is more rigorous than for any other group of immigrants, lasting up to two years, but some governors have refused to settle them in their states.

Anyone who applies for United States citizenship has to answer various questions about the Declaration of Independence.

★ ★ ★ ★ ★ ★ ★ ★ ★ ★ ★ ★ ★ ★ ★ ★

WISE WORDS

"Our forefathers understood the very nature and need for our nation to replenish itself through future immigration. . . . We are told by our founders that we must endeavor to encourage migration to our exceptional nation. That is part and parcel of . . . our Declaration of Independence."

—Robert Gittelson,
President of Conservatives for Comprehensive Immigration Reform

★ ★ ★ ★ ★ ★ ★ ★ ★ ★ ★ ★ ★ ★ ★ ★

Not to Be Taken for Granted

The Declaration can be easy for Americans to take for granted—but this isn't the case elsewhere. This—the first time a colony had successfully broken free of its ruler— launched similar movements around the world.

"The independence of the Anglo-Americans," raved a French scholar in 1787, "is the event most likely to accelerate the revolution that must bring happiness on earth."

The scholar's fervor might be overly optimistic. But within fifty years of ours, at least twenty other Declarations of Independence appeared. It was quoted with enthusiasm during the French Revolution (1789–1799), encouraged those trying to overthrow the Spanish empire in South America (late eighteenth and early nineteenth centuries), and inspired revolts elsewhere.

With the tumult of World War I, it was again in the spotlight. Within a few years of one another, from 1916 to 1919, Korea, Czechoslovakia, Ireland, and Estonia all wrote their own Declarations of Independence.

It again became especially relevant after the end of World War II in 1945, with a new emphasis on human rights tying in so well to the Declaration's language. Colonization was starting to break down everywhere around the world, with more people standing up for themselves and against their rulers. In particular, leaders of independence movements against the British Empire in India (achieved in 1947) and elsewhere used the American Revolution as their model.

★ ★ ★ ★ ★ ★ ★ ★ ★ ★ ★ ★ ★ ★ ★ ★

WISE WORDS

"The Declaration of Independence and its historically revolutionary affirmation of human equality have uplifted and inspired hundreds of millions of people globally of all races and ethnicities."

—author Mark D. Tooley

★ ★ ★ ★ ★ ★ ★ ★ ★ ★ ★ ★ ★ ★ ★ ★

And again it renewed its fame in the 1990s, after the breakup of the Soviet Union led to the creation of many independent countries.

Today well over half of the countries around the world have their own Declarations of Independence—all derived from ours.

One hundred years after our war, a historian named George Trevelyan wrote, "It may be doubted whether so small a number of men ever employed so short a space of time with greater and more lasting effects upon the history of the world."

In other words, the American Revolution had changed everything.

Selected Sources

Albert H. Small Declaration of Independence Collection, University of Virginia Library, http://small.library.virginia. edu/collections/featured/albert-h-small-declaration-of-independence-collection/

Archer, Jules. *They Made a Revolution: The Sons and Daughters of the American Revolution*, foreword by Kathleen Krull. New York: Sky Pony Press, 2016.

Armitage, David. *The Declaration of Independence: A Global History*. Cambridge: Harvard University Press, 2007.

Brown, Richard H., and Paul E. Cohen. *Revolution: Mapping the Road to American Independence 1755–1783*. New York: Norton, 2015.

Campaign 1776, www.campaign1776.org/revolutionary-war/

Casey, Susan. *Women Heroes of the American Revolution: 20 Stories of Espionage, Sabotage, Defiance, and Rescue*. Chicago: Chicago Review Press, 2015.

Declaration of Independence, full text, www.archives.gov/ exhibits/charters/declaration_transcript.html

Dunbar-Ortiz, Roxanne. *An Indigenous Peoples' History of the United States*. Boston: Beacon Press, 2015.

Dupont, Christian Y., and Peter S. Onuf, eds. *Declaring Independence: The Origin and Influence of America's Founding Document*. Charlottesville, VA.: University of Virginia Library, 2010, revised edition.

DuVal, Kathleen. *Independence Lost: Lives on the Edge of the American Revolution*. New York: Random House, 2015.

George Washington Digital Encyclopedia, www.mountvernon. org/digital-encyclopedia/

Hadlow, Janice. *A Royal Experiment: The Private Life of King George III*. New York: Holt, 2014.

Hakim, Joy. *A History of Us: From Colonies to Country*. New York: Oxford University Press, 1993.

Hogeland, William. *Declaration: The Nine Tumultuous Weeks When America Became Independent, May 1-July 4, 1776*. New York: Simon & Schuster, 2010.

Independence National Historical Park, www.nps.gov/inde/index. htm

Journal of the American Revolution Teacher's Guide, https:// allthingsliberty.com/teachers-guide/

Krensky, Stephen. *The Declaration of Independence*. New York: Cavendish Square, 2011.

Krull, Kathleen. *A Kids' Guide to America's Bill of Rights*. New York: Harper, 2015, revised edition.

——*What Was the Boston Tea Party?* New York: Grosset & Dunlap, 2013.

Maier, Pauline. *American Scripture: Making the Declaration of Independence*. New York: Knopf, 1997.

Marcovitz, Hal. *The Declaration of Independence: Forming a New Nation*. Broomall, PA: Mason Crest, 2014.

Museum of the American Revolution, www.amrevmuseum.org.

Nash, Gary B. *The Forgotten Fifth: African Americans in the Age of Revolution*. Cambridge: Harvard University Press, 2006

Raphael, Ray and Marie. *The Spirit of '74: How the American Revolution Began*. New York: The New Press, 2015.

Redmond, Shirley Raye. *Patriots in Petticoats: Heroines of the American Revolution*. New York: Random, 2004

Revolution250, www.revolution250.org

Schama, Simon. *Rough Crossings: Britain, the Slaves, and the American Revolution*. New York: HarperCollins, 2006.

Sheinkin, Steve. *King George: What Was His Problem?* New York: Roaring Brook, 2008.

The American Revolution, 1763-1783, The Gilder Lehrman

Institute of American History, www.gilderlehrman.org/
history-by-era/american-revolution-1763-1783

The Declaration of Independence, www.ushistory.org/declaration/
index.htm

Yero, Judith Lloyd. *The Declaration of Independence*. Washington,
DC: National Geographic, 2006.

Young, Alfred F. *Masquerade: The Life and Times of Deborah
Sampson, Continental Soldier*. New York: Knopf, 2004.

Index

Read them all!